STOP
FIXING
WOMEN

CATHERINE FOX is one of Australia's leading commentators on women and the workforce. She wrote the 'Corporate Woman' column for the *Australian Financial Review* for many years and has written three previous books, including *Seven Myths about Women and Work* (NewSouth), which was shortlisted for the 2013 Ashurst Business Literature Prize. She helped establish the annual Westpac/Financial Review 100 Women of Influence Awards and is on several advisory boards, including the Australian Defence Force Gender Equality Advisory Board.

STOP FIXING WOMEN

Why building fairer workplaces is everyone's business

CATHERINE FOX

NEWSOUTH

To David: for supporting, not fixing.

A NewSouth book

Published by
NewSouth Publishing
University of New South Wales Press Ltd
University of New South Wales
Sydney NSW 2052
AUSTRALIA
newsouthpublishing.com

National Library of Australia
Cataloguing-in-Publication entry
Creator: Fox, Catherine (Catherine Louise), author.
Title: Stop fixing women / Catherine Fox.
ISBN: 9781742235165 (paperback)
        9781742242798 (ebook)
        9781742248264 (epdf)
Subjects: Women's rights.
Women – Employment.
Quality of work life.
Sex discrimination against women.
Gender identity.
Equality.

Design Jo Pajor-Markus
Cover design Alissa Dinallo
Printer Griffin Press

Contents

Introduction

'I am the generic person. I am a
middle-class white man. I have no race,
no class, no gender. I am universally
generalisable.'

Michael Kimmel[1]

IN 2015, A GROUP OF the corporate elite gathered in the heartland of Sydney's business district to launch another initiative designed to open boardroom doors to more women. It could just as well have been London, New York or Toronto. And in fact this particular program for women was originally launched in the UK.

A panel of distinguished businessmen took to to the stage to discuss why more women were needed on boards, and their support for this program to speed up the process. The conversation went along fairly predictably until a few comments began to make it clear that many of these 'supporters' have deep-seated concerns about the capacity and appetite of women for these sought-after seats at the table. It's a fact that women don't put their hand up for promotions as often as men, said one. Appointing a woman with no listed board experience is a risk, said another, and then quickly rephrased to include 'anyone' without that experience. The woman sitting next to me, a senior executive and director, leant over and whispered, 'They are blaming us'.

She was right, they were. I've heard so much of this scapegoating and observed the wilful blindness about the other side of the equation – the behaviour and attitudes of those who still hold most of the power – that even I had become a little desensitised. A few months later I was on stage discussing these issues in front of an audience of mid-career female managers alongside a senior male bureaucrat and a female executive. The man talked convincingly about the need for more women in his workforce but soon began telling the group, who had given up time and money to be there, they needed to think about 'backing themselves'. I could see the 'Here we go again' expressions on many faces. Why would they even be there if they didn't back themselves? I did point out the unhelpful nature of this type of advice, but I'm not sure my fellow speaker appreciated it.

Telling women it's mostly their own fault for being marginalised in workplaces designed by and for male breadwinners – and failing to crack through the glass ceiling and scale the ranks of business – reinforces ridiculously outdated gender stereotypes. We used to call this the 'deficit model', because it rests on the belief that women are naturally deficient in risk taking, assertiveness and courage, while being over-endowed with emotions and caring skills. Many of us, me included, thought this idea had started to disappear, but I think we were wrong. The workplace rhetoric might be more about how men and women have 'different' skills these days, but that hasn't changed the thinking. For 'different' read 'mostly faulty' – the 'Women need fixing' message is as strong as ever.

It's illogical too. How can women be both the problem and the solution when they make up just under half the workforce but still a tiny minority of decision makers? As I looked more deeply into this I realised how horribly effective this approach can be in corroding women's status and distracting organisations from taking on the real culprits. And in case a reminder is needed, dismantling inequity is far from some 'politically correct', feel-good exercise. More equal societies score more highly on just about every economic and social indicator there is, and they are more productive and happier too. There is a clear correlation between gender equality and GDP per capita, the level of economic competitiveness and human development, according to the World Economic Forum.[2] To put it another way, a 6 per cent increase in participation in the workforce by Australian women could add $25 billion to GDP, according to the Grattan Institute.[3]

Compelling stuff, but apparently not a pressing concern for many who have been holding the reins. But it has become much clearer to me through my analysis that the focus on fixing women has also been very handy in allowing men, and particularly powerful men, to stay out of the debate. After all, if women's lack of skills is to blame for them failing to thrive, then it's obviously up to them to remedy this deficiency. And it's their fault when the latest 'diversity' program doesn't make much difference. But if the bias and unfairness is not only about the personal but the political – the way workplaces are run and by whom – then the people with power, who are overwhelmingly privileged white middle-aged men, are not just nice to have on side. They are essential to success. They not only have to stand up as advocates but they must change the rules and norms that helped give them a big advantage in getting the keys to the top office.

That uncomfortable realisation is dawning but it's a tough grind to challenge the establishment – and particularly when you're facing a tsunami of advice that all it takes is fixing women. There's an industry churning out advice books and consulting services, sometimes produced by women, who also lap up this stuff. It's appealing because it promises a quick fix. And plenty of women get quite tetchy about dismantling the deficit model, and tell me they see evidence of low confidence and poor negotiating skills from women all the time, so isn't it better to arm them with tips to help them?

Well, if women really needed fixing because of their gender, and these tips helped to change the real causes of discrimination, then yes it would be. But I don't think they do, or that packaged 'remedies' have delivered results – but I often see them reinforcing the stereotypes that are the problem in the first place. Fans of remedial 'solutions' spend plenty of time promoting research that says women aren't feisty enough, but turn a blind eye to the studies (many cited in this book) showing the role of context and socialisation – not biology – in shaping these responses, and showing that putting the onus on individuals (and only half the workforce at that) to fix major structural problems doesn't work. Many of the commonly quoted pitfalls for women (such as putting a hand up for a job or speaking up at meetings) are exaggerated, but such responses would decline if there were, say, less biased rules and self-fulfilling assumptions about gender. And telling women to essentially behave 'like men' backfires spectacularly and not just for women. Remember the follies of over-confident 'Masters of the Universe' bankers in the lead-up to the global financial crisis? Dismantling the remedial model for women leads us to examine the other side: the pervasive belief that stereotypical masculine behaviour should be the standard for all. Such scrutiny is long overdue.

So here's what I've set out to do: to analyse why we have continued down the slippery and counterproductive slope of blaming women for structural sexism and what that means, and to advocate for an urgent shift that dumps the deficit and includes men – yes, all men – in tackling new norms if we are to finally make some progress. My guiding themes are that women are not wired for inadequacy but are coping with routine bias and sexism, while the men who still hold the power to set the norms, behaviours and attitudes prevailing in workplaces therefore need to help change them.

There are many wise and wonderful women who have helped me shape my thoughts. But who better to also include in this endeavour than the small but growing cohort of male leaders stepping into a space they usually fear to tread? After years of token gender rhetoric and passive platitudes about the problem-solving itself, some are now making the transfer from being bystanders to supporters in addressing gender equality. I was already familiar with some of the work being done in organisations such as Telstra, the Treasury and Aurizon. But my research shows that successful interventions in a range of companies, government departments and the small business sector have a common theme: they focus on how workplaces, not women, are operating. I have used examples I found compelling and that could pass the credibility test. Not every sector is covered – and there will be organisations doing terrific work that I have not included. But my choices are practical and I hope insightful, rather than an attempt to be comprehensive.

Not all CEOs practise what they preach, as I know only too well. But there are others who are gradually learning to 'check their privilege', as the Americans might put it, and increasingly stepping into the gender space. Some, though by no means all, are members of a group set up in Australia, the Male Champions of Change (MCC), which has been growing. The 'men for women' trend has not been without controversy and many object to the patriarchal symbolism. Yes, it's a lot of talk and not enough action yet. Then of course there are the examples – there will be more to come, I suspect – of organisations saying one thing on diversity but apparently doing another. As I was writing this book ANZ, which I have included as an example of progress particularly for its work on superannuation for female employees, faced allegations of blatant sexism by former traders in the dealing room (the unfair dismissal action taken by these two men was later dropped). These contradictions can't be denied but they can be used as incentives, and several MCC members told me nobody wants to be ridiculed for hypocrisy. That's a strong motivation to get your house in order and many are very aware they are a long way from that yet.

My aim is not to congratulate these men nor other male advocates but to encourage them to work harder and get the message to their male peers and employees. Women walk a tightrope as supporters of gender equity, pilloried both for 'playing the victim' and for not speaking up enough. Acting on their own, women were never going to shift the status quo without getting those men at the top to recognise there is a serious business and workforce problem to confront, as even a cursory look at the data from the past two decades makes clear.

I've been following the statistics and the debate for decades. I wrote the *Australian Financial Review*'s 'Corporate Woman' column on and off from 1992 to 2012. In the early days of my stint, women's sections in the media were still mainly full of recipes and style tips. And it was long before the Huffington Post or Mamamia or other women's sites started – well before use of the internet was widespread, in fact. In those days my beat was a fairly lonely one and tended to cover reporting on overt discrimination. These were the routine cases of women being sacked if they announced they were pregnant, or wanted a change to their work schedule to help with childcare obligations. Or there were the job interviews at an airline where women were asked to sing and dance, in the days when flight attendants were still called air hostesses. I never heard of male flight attendants being asked to jump through that particular hoop.

It was also commonplace to hear that women lacked the 'get up and go' to make it up the ladder or stick it out. They didn't want the senior jobs, I was frequently told by the men who were tenaciously holding onto these plum roles: that was the main reason women were rare in those corner offices. It was a rationale that felt comfortable and let the men in charge off the hook. Nevertheless, I watched and hoped as more and more hardy women slowly fought their way onto building sites; became firefighters, doctors and dentists; climbed the ranks and busted a stack of myths that women can't build careers or work as hard as men because they lack ambition and have children. Surely this would change the ground rules and prove once and for all that women are fully human and just as able and competent as men? I was wrong about that. Yes, the world has changed, but some fundamental stories we tell to explain key areas of gender inequality have not, and nor have the outcomes.

From fundamental rights to fair pay and conditions to shattering that glass ceiling – better described as a thick layer of men, according to US feminist Laura Liswood – there is much to be done. We know nearly 50 per cent of the paid workforce is female in many parts of the world (in Australia it's 47 per cent). Australian women's labour force participation, according to the Australian Bureau of Statistics, has increased slightly over the past decade, from 58 per cent to 59 per cent, while men's participation has remained largely stable at around 71 per cent. But the pay gap between men and women sits at close to 18 per cent in many countries. Almost 35 per cent of Australian women have no superannuation.[4] Most women who will retire in the next 20 years don't even have enough for a modest retirement – 55 per cent of women aged 45 to 54 had less than $25 000 in superannuation in 2009–2010. From the age of 35 until retirement, a woman's superannuation balance will typically be half that of a man the same age.

These are big problems for economies globally. But the composition of groups making fundamental decisions that affect every one of these areas remains stubbornly male. Move up the ranks of just about any company and the proportion of women rapidly shrinks to much less than half. There are just 23 per cent women on the top 200 listed Australian company boards (and that is a major improvement from 2009, when there were 8 per cent), and women make up only 26 per cent of key management personnel, and 17 per cent of CEOs across the business sector (according to Workplace Gender Equality Agency data). Women run around a third of small businesses in Australia, and it is estimated that just 4.3 per cent of Australian tech start-up companies were founded by women, although that figure rises to 25 per cent of total start-ups.[5] In the Australian Defence Force (ADF), a strong focus on attracting and retaining women has seen a modest increase of just 1 per cent, to 15.1 per cent, in the past few years. And worldwide, the cohort of new CEOs appointed in 2015 were more male than in previous years.[6] Just 3 per cent of new CEO hires were women in 2015, compared to 5 per cent in 2014. And the ratio was worst in North America and Canada, where just one new incoming CEO out of 87 was a woman. In its 2016 report on women and work, consulting firm McKinsey found women remain underrepresented at every level in the corporate pipeline. Corporate America promotes men at 30 per cent higher rates than women during the early stages of their careers; women negotiate for promotions and raises as often as men but face more pushback when they do. And the challenges are even more pronounced for women of colour.[7]

No wonder there's been a tendency for 'gender fatigue' – a lack of energy to tackle a seemingly intractable problem – to set in, or for window dressing by pointing to actions rather than outcomes, sometimes described as gender washing. That sham is particularly frustrating when there's still such a lot that can be done. You don't start challenging established narratives and power structures without paying a price, however. There's a ferocious level of backlash seething below the formal rhetoric about gender equality in workplaces. It's vicious and ugly, and can be personally damaging for those who speak up, but it has to be acknowledged and tackled too – by both men and women. The savage attacks on women in the social media sphere have become topical, but it's not just happening in cyberspace.

The young students who set up a cupcake stall at University of Queensland in early 2016 and charged women less for the cakes to reflect the gender pay gap attracted an astonishing level of vitriol. There were calls to physically attack the students, vehement denials of any pay gap, and talk about the need for 'feminazis' to be eradicated. And these were attacks on mostly young women of privilege – the impact of such vitriolic sexism is even more pronounced for women from non-Anglo Saxon backgrounds or those who struggle to access education and employment. It's still the case that many discussions around gender equity at work focus on white professionals, which hardly reflects the community we live in and risks ignoring the crucial and toxic interplay of racism and sexism. The term 'intersectionality' was coined by American civil rights advocate and scholar, Kimberlé Williams Crenshaw, to describe the ways in which different forms of oppression are interconnected and cannot be examined separately from one another.[8]

Given these issues, it is important to clarify that my analysis and criticism of the deficit model has ramifications for all women, from those in low-skilled jobs to professionals, and the examples here range from the big end of town to the military. The progress being made – such as topping up low-level superannuation accounts for female employees at ANZ (see chapter 4) – comes from both grass roots activism and concerted action at the top.

And refocusing this debate is not about giving women a 'get out of jail free card' or painting them as victims. Many women now have more personal agency over how they live and work than a generation ago and are well aware they are responsible for their own progress. But the deficit model means women are facing an extra range of hampering assumptions about their abilities that imply they must try harder to get the same outcomes as their male peers. They don't need to be fixed but like all employees, they need support and advice in navigating workplaces. To stop fixing women is not to suggest women are flawless either. I have long argued that portraying women as 'better' than men with a set of special nurturing abilities is reinforcing unhelpful stereotypes (and the same goes for norms that paint men as inept carers). The problem is the dependence on broad gender stereotypes to explain inequality effectively prevents women from accessing the same range of options as men at home and in their paid work, whether they are low skilled or well educated. It means their expertise and behaviour are judged and valued differently. It also leaves male norms at work largely unchallenged.

Many strong voices in this debate – Australia's current and former Sex Discrimination Commissioners Kate Jenkins and Elizabeth Broderick, former Governor-General Quentin Bryce, feminist Wendy McCarthy, journalist Annabel Crabb, Sydney University economist Marian Baird, the iconic Gloria Steinem and US academic Anne-Marie Slaughter – have called for men to be partners in changing how we work and live so there is greater fairness. In her book *Unfinished Business*, Slaughter argues compellingly for refocusing on the conflict between care and competition in modern societies rather than on women and work in order to trigger real change. As long as this dichotomy is in place, the intense labour of tending to home and family will be seen as women's work and the paid and powerful jobs will be regarded as men's, she argues.

To change the division of labour and revalue family work, I believe we need to shift expectations and the structure of paid jobs, and redefine what a 'successful' working life means for men and women. That's been my focus as a business journalist and reinforced my firm belief that the workplace is a fulcrum for fundamental change and, ideally, improvement in the status of women. My last book, *7 myths about women and work*, set out some of the commonly held assumptions and stereotypes that hinder women, in the workplace and in society. It certainly hit the mark in many workplaces and triggered some lively discussions at forums.

But just as importantly, readers such as the chief of the Australian Army at the time, David Morrison, found analysis of the myths a help in devising and implementing some major changes in the army as he engaged deeply with the problem. In his now-famous speech, following a series of sexual harassment incidents in the army, he memorably told his troops: 'On all operations, female soldiers and officers have proven themselves worthy of the best traditions of the Australian Army. They are vital to us, maintaining our capability now and into the future. If that does not suit you, then get out! You may find another employer where your attitude and behaviour is acceptable, but I doubt it.'

But some years on, it feels like the time is right to go a step further and look at what links the myths and who is actually making headway in tackling these well-documented barriers.

Some of the interventions I've described here are occurring in surprising settings. Who knew the army could be run by a man who sounds a lot like a feminist? But many of these strategies will not automatically convince those who have benefited from the existing structures to suddenly ask the women they work with to take away some of their power and money. I can't see any profound changes in the way we work – paid and unpaid – occurring unless these interventions actually spread and are seen as business imperatives by more leaders.

Immersing myself in this work has left me astonished at how many of the key areas of gender inequality have continued to be framed as women's problems while ignoring the impact of the biased rules – and the attitudes and behaviour of the men who make up the other half of the workforce. Why, for example, do we still tell women their negotiating skills or failure to ask for more is the reason for the gender pay gap when the data clearly shows that after just one year in the workforce male and female graduates on average are paid differently? And girls get less pocket money than boys? How many women even get to negotiate their pay? And what about examining the way performance and potential is judged, particularly by male managers? Far too often, when we talk about what's normal in workplaces, it's about what men in the mainstream do; when we talk about gender, it's about women. Many men still don't even see themselves as having a gender, as US academic Michael Kimmel says.

No wonder the easiest solution seems to be all about fitting women into male shoes. To call this counterproductive is being generous. Instead of ignoring the male side of the equation, it's time to get them enlisted to change the picture. Obsessing about fixing women has been part of the problem and a brake on gender equity progress, socially and economically. Enlist alpha males in examining the power equation and workplace norms and you have a chance of effectively reframing both the causes of and solutions to unfairness. Because here's what has become obvious to me: when they talk about changing the system, these men are in fact talking about changing themselves. They are the system.

CHAPTER 1

From victim blaming to system shaming

> 'Men invented the system.
> Men largely run the system. Men need
> to change the system.'
>
> GORDON CAIRNS, NON-EXECUTIVE DIRECTOR, CHAIR, WOOLWORTHS LTD[1]

AT THE END OF 2011 I got a call from the Sex Discrimination Commissioner, Elizabeth Broderick, who had just been at a meeting in Canberra with the head of the Australian Treasury, Martin Parkinson. They'd been discussing a major review of how women fared in one of the nation's most powerful and prestigious departments, and he was happy to discuss the findings and the plans to address them with me, she said. The interview a day or two later was fascinating, and not quite what I expected from one of the more influential mandarins in Australia. Instead of the usual defensiveness, denial or victim blaming and bland platitudes about doing better, Parkinson said the findings of the detailed and candid review by consultant Deborah May had set off loud alarm bells through the organisation.

He admitted that for years he'd believed that the discrepancies in gender numbers in the upper ranks of the department were mainly the result of childbearing breaks and care responsibilities shouldered by women. Like many of his peers, he said it really didn't occur to him that there could be covert or indeed even overt bias to blame for the lack of women making it through. Treasury, after all, is an enclave of the smartest people in the country, who pride themselves on excellent analytical skills. Surely they couldn't be missing something quite fundamental – and detrimental – about how their workplace operated?

As it turned out, many of the senior bureaucrats had indeed been blind to this. And Parkinson came to see he had been missing a key factor. 'I had a light bulb moment: that we were treating the symptoms and not the cause. I had thought the barriers for women were self-resolving.'

There's a slightly donnish quality about Parkinson, although much of his career has been spent in the top enclaves of government. At a launch of a case study about the gender work done at Treasury in Parliament House, he revealed he was raised in his early years by his grandmother, while his mother worked to support the household. It's clear that along with a growing awareness of the breadth of the issue, he also has a strong personal motivation for seeing better outcomes for women. In 1997 Parkinson joined the IMF before returning to Treasury in

2001. At that time he realised that the rate of female progression hadn't changed much despite a decade of recruiting high levels of female graduates. But there was a reasonable spread of women across the department, and again he thought that time would see these discrepancies resolved. The problem, he thought, would fix itself.

In 2011, he again returned to Treasury after establishing and leading the Department of Climate Change. After a major study on gender in the department, he knew that expecting a change to the status quo without action was a mistake and too convenient an explanation which didn't address the significantly lower numbers of women in many parts of Treasury from early on in their careers. The organisation had indeed focused on addressing the symptoms, not the underlying problem. There were systemic issues and Parkinson and his team set about tackling them using the review findings, which he admits were tough to read. 'I remember very clearly hearing Deb's findings with my Executive Board, and Nigel Ray, Deputy Secretary of the Macroeconomic Group, turned to the group and said, "We are not leading the organisation we thought we were leading"', Parkinson recalls. 'The Executive Board was bound together on this issue from that moment onwards.'

Treasury went on to release information about pay, recruitment and progression. Individual groups in the department reported on their own data – interview rates, conversion rates to appointments and so on, with Parkinson telling interview committees not to stop at advertising vacancies but to actively seek out the best candidates for them. Nigel Ray adopted the '50:50: If not why not?' initiative and encouraged women to put themselves forward for roles.

The results began to emerge shortly afterwards. Dubbed the Progressing Women Initiative (PWI), the program includes gender audits, unconscious bias training, making managers accountable to gender targets, improving flexible working arrangements, and creating a senior diversity committee. It saw female representation in senior executive roles rise from 22 per cent to 33 per cent in three years to 2014, although the level dropped to 28.6 per cent by mid-2015 (according to the 2014/15 annual report). Women made up 51.5 per cent of Treasury's workforce in mid-June 2015, an increase from 50.6 per cent a year before. In 2015 Parkinson was appointed to run the Department of Prime Minister and Cabinet and there are plans to use his PWI framework as a model to be rolled out across the public sector. His successor at Treasury, John Fraser, however decided not to join the MCC.[2]

There are many reasons why the Treasury under Parkinson and his team was able to make such a shift in operations and rules to change the gender ratio in the organisation. An important factor was that the men running the department underwent a reality check about what was actually happening in their own workplace rather than what they thought was occurring. Making powerful men advocates for women's empowerment has been equally cheered and jeered in recent years but it is an approach that rests on some fundamental logic: many female flag bearers for gender equality have long attempted to have their concerns taken seriously by the men running organisations. Their efforts were of course necessary and steadfast but not sufficient – you only have to look at the sobering list of statistics that haven't budged to know that this challenge rarely made it to the serious business agenda. A circuit breaker was needed.

That was one of the reasons the Male Champions of Change, which Parkinson belongs to, was formed by Elizabeth Broderick in 2010 when she was Sex Discrimination Commissioner. Although he was ambivalent about the all-male membership, Parkinson said the rationale made sense. 'It's men who are in power positions; if you can't get a bunch of men to talk to other men about this, why would we believe the pace of change can be any different? For me it was very much a sense that we needed to be seen as stepping up alongside women, and as men trying to fix the system by trying to do the right thing. That's why it has been so important to work with (membership body) Chief Executive Women on the core strategy.'

When I asked her about the thinking behind the group, Broderick explained why relying on women alone to solve the under-representation of women at the leadership level is illogical. 'Women by and large do not hold the levers of power. If this issue is allowed to sit squarely on the shoulders of women alone, any failure to make progress will also be laid at their feet. Not only that, but progress will remain painfully slow. That is why blaming women for the lack of progress is not only unfair, it's also unhelpful. Gender equality is not a women's issue. It's an economic and societal issue, one that affects all of us.'

As she also points out, the structures holding women back are part of a system that is deeply rooted in a male way of being – which means men, and particularly powerful men, need to use that clout to create change. 'They represent the system. I was recently asked by a man, "Well, who will speak for me, a white Anglo-Saxon Christian man?" My response was, "You are the system; your voice, your views are crowding out every other voice. That's why we need you to take the message of gender equality to every other man".' And Broderick is well aware that it's much easier to focus on fixing women to fit into this existing power model, because that's been the comfortable alternative for most organisations from the year dot. Fixing the system requires men to step up beside women as equal partners in change. And while she sees this happening more and more, there's still a way to go in building a critical mass of men as equal partners in reform.

The men who are on board have begun to understand how crucial it is to switch from seeing gender balance as a women's problem to seeing it a workplace issue, and that at its heart, this is about who has access to power. That shift gets some momentum from analysing and challenging the deficit model. When organisational thinking doesn't concentrate on how women fail to match masculine norms, then the steps to address bias start to look rather different. The approaches can broaden out and away from tinkering with measures for women, such as the 'mummy track' of part-time work (which I will examine in the next chapter), or sending women on remedial programs to hone those networking skills or boost confidence. This is sometimes called the 'sheep dip method', as it involves dunking women into training and expecting them to come out the other end magically transformed.

But no amount of sheep dipping will alter the beliefs of leaders who have traditional values and rely on stereotypes, particularly when it comes to the vexed question of merit and who should be the boss (more on this in chapter 3). To do that there has to be a focus on identifying and changing the norms, practices and policies that fail the fairness test and don't match today's workforce demands. As the work of Parkinson and his colleagues makes clear, that kind of action is now being initiated by male leaders. That is a radical change from a few years ago – and the thinking is catching on.

I've known consultant Deborah May, who produced the review of women in Treasury, for many years and seen her effectively provide detailed workplace analysis to kickstart this process. Her work in Treasury is just part of a number of projects with a range of government agencies to help their senior echelons – mainly men – to understand how organisational norms can stymie women. 'I think it's the culture which is central and behaviours – how we do things around here – and the more we understand that, and the fact it sometimes doesn't work, the better.'

May begins her projects by asking questions – lots of them – that focus not on women but on the organisation's workplace culture, and the informal rules that work to the advantage of men but to the disadvantage of women. Her work with Treasury found there were two clear factors at play that disadvantaged women. 'One was the allocation of work, which meant that women were assigned organisational relationship and coordination roles and men were given hardcore economic analysis. Even though they had the same qualifications from day one. In addition to that, the cultural norms of "how we do things around here" that were recognised and rewarded were clear.'

The behaviours that ticked boxes and were therefore rewarded were direct communication styles, decisiveness and being seen as authoritative. What didn't get rewarded was being seen as too consultative and not knowing the answer. No prizes for guessing that the two styles split pretty neatly into what was perceived as a male versus a female approach. Further analysis

found the policies and practices within Treasury such as performance management systems were subtly penalising women
because they had (or were believed to have) a different interpre-
tation or way of exhibiting conceptual and analytical skills – the
most crucial performance factors in the organisation. There was
a level of unconscious bias, May says, but the bias was grounded
in the system.

These findings had an effect on how certain responsibilities were distributed to men and women from early on in their
careers. The department now puts young men into the co-ordi-
nation roles once deemed more suitable for women – and there
is increased recognition of the impact of these decisions and
more conscious changes as a result, she says. The penny has been
dropping in all sorts of ways: it's not just recognising the pattern
of who gets a role, but how that work allocation gets in the way
of progression. And May says helping people start to see themselves and their culture through the eyes of others is pivotal to
change. She usually spends half a day with women when running workshops to normalise their experience and help them
to understand the way bias in practice operates. A core message
to women is 'It's not about them and it's not because they are
incompetent'.

At the Department of Foreign Affairs and Trade the problems with systemic bias were more about career paths and attitudes to flexible work, particularly how and whether part-time
work could be arranged, May explains. Given this is a workplace
where overseas postings are part and parcel of many careers and
jobs, the whole issue of flexible work becomes a crucial differ-
entiator between the up-and-comers and those heading for the
career cul de sac. In the past there was not really any such thing

as flexible work and if you didn't get a posting you were in trouble. Some women told May they felt their careers were over: they had to make a choice between having a career or a family.

The new approach to flexible work and parental leave in the department was about tackling the systemic bias that saw senior managers reluctant to put people into part-time roles and therefore left many women unable to progress. Development and training were other areas where problems would arise for women, May says, particularly with secondments and high-visibility roles where careers are often forged. But it's not enough to recognise the problem – action has to be planned and executed. A strong leader makes all the difference – and luckily more men are stepping up to the task, given they continue to run the majority of organisations in most parts of the world.

Treasury and the Department of Foreign Affairs and Trade are quite different environments to the workplace at Aurizon, the former Queensland Rail. The traditional transport and freight company is a major listed company employing nearly 7000 workers, of which 16 per cent were women in 2015 – not too many of whom are driving the trains, although that is changing. The CEO for six years until late 2016, Lance Hockridge, is a former BHP executive, and has been a champion of better gender balance for many years. He publicly made a commitment to have 30 per cent of the Aurizon workforce made up of women by the end of 2019 and his active interventions – as he calls the changes he is making – are quoted throughout this book. We sat down to chat in early 2016 and he says that while the battle for more progress with women continues, there is a change in attitudes and a growing sense this is no passing fad.

'It's way too early to declare victory but there's a sense of having taken hold. It's a cultural journey but accompanied by a broad range of processes. Over the last twelve months one of the more significant things has been the impact of the internal male Champions of Change Group – it started out with a dozen people and it got to twenty-four and it was voluntary, having gone around and tapped people on the shoulder originally. What it has done is to take a decision that it's a twelve-month tenure and then they get a whole new group that will be appointed. This year they are running a series of programs in the culture space, and last year they did a survey on what was women's experience and that got some good stuff.'

But it also picked up on some not such good stuff too, Hockridge adds. Disturbingly, some of the attitudes the company would have liked to think had long since disappeared were still around – that women should be seen and not heard, questioning why women were being appointed to senior roles when they will just go off and have babies, a woman in a meeting is there to take notes, and so it went on. 'There were still entrenched stereotypes and we've launched a "Stand Up and Speak Up" campaign and the first part of that is encouraging people to ask "What did you mean by that?"', he says. The idea is to give permission for a response when poor behaviour or passive-aggressive comments are made and to try and tackle the bystander syndrome – that is, that the standard you walk past is the standard you accept. It's starting to have an effect and is part of legitimising doing the right thing but it will be a while before the impact can be measured. 'The power of 150 years of culture will not change by simply doing the right thing and having the right recruitment processes – that's not what will make the big difference.'

'It may be important to change some of the formal rules but you also have to intervene and that's at the heart of where Aurizon is at, driving the different approach, and it will create discontent and dislocation but the men in the organisation have run the rails for 150 years and all we are doing is creating some balance', says Hockridge. Driving trains is not assumed to be a woman's job. But Aurizon has found there is no difference in the skills of female drivers when compared to male drivers, and similarly to the mining companies, there have been benefits from the way women use more care in running the machinery, with the upshot that having women in the role has 'lifted the game for everybody'.

Parkinson and Hockridge have both made a commitment to publish results but also accepted that many of their colleagues will find the changes confronting and upsetting. Some will be hoping the wave of changes is a passing phase and a bit of 'political correctness' gone awry. That's certainly a belief in parts of the Australian Defence Force (examined in chapter 7). But they are realistic and firmly reject the idea that their actions are part of a fad. And they both credit the membership of the Male Champions of Change with giving them some extra support in their work.

The group model has been found to provide some import-ant benefits, according to Melbourne Business School Professor Isabel Metz, who interviewed many of the members for a 2016 research paper.[3] She found the motivation for joining varied but was more likely to be personal than external. Men who were passionate about gender equity were likely to be active support-ers of change. The rest were best described as bystanders but some of them become quite passionate about gender equity after joining, as their understanding of the issue increases, she found. The secret to continued impact is finding and keeping those passionate leaders who commit time and financial resources, are prepared to be public advocates, and understand that this is a long-term commitment with lots of upside but also plenty of downside. And sometimes you need to get the men in the room to discover why just having men in the room is not working – as Ken Morrison, the CEO of the Property Council and a member of the Property MCC (chaired by businesswoman Carol Schwartz) explained, one of their stated goals is indeed breaking up the boys' club.

The MCC are not the only men standing up for better gender equality. But data on the group helps reveal a little about the motivation for this advocacy – which is both for business and personal reasons, as Metz discovered in her research. Some are also at a stage in their careers where they want to leave a legacy that is not just about the bottom line. Some have told me they now see these steps as being long overdue – like the Canadian Prime Minister Justin Trudeau, who when asked why he prioritised having 50 per cent women in his cabinet replied, 'Because it's 2015'. Many have seen the need for change in their own families, as their wives and daughters face barriers in the workforce.

There are of course many other examples, some from unlikely sectors, where the same realisation is dawning, backed by a groundswell of support from the broader community. Driving home one day in 2016 I heard a news bulletin announcing that Australian sports bodies would have to ensure they had gender-neutral travel policies for men and women. Not long before there had been an outcry when it was revealed the

Australian men's football team, the Socceroos, got to travel in business seats while the women's team, the Matildas, were relegated to cattle class. Not a good look. Federal sports minister Sussan Ley and Australian Sports Commission (ASC) chairman John Wylie wrote to the 30 top funded sports organisations, setting out their expectations for change. 'In 2016, we can think of no defensible reason why male and female athletes should travel in different classes or stay in different standard accommodation when attending major international sporting events', the letter reads. 'The ASC is now proposing to make gender-neutral travel policies for senior major championships a condition of investment by the ASC in a sport.' The ASC provides $134 million in funding to different sporting organisations a year in a sport-obsessed nation, which gives the body plenty of informal leverage with the different codes. The Minister rather cleverly avoided a mandate to the sports bodies and announced there was to be naming and shaming of poor performers, but said she was 'confident public pressure would bring about change'.[4]

Sport is certainly a big deal in Australian society, and sports stars are often seen as iconic heroes who help define our national identity. That means efforts to challenge the male domination of iconic codes – rugby, cricket and AFL – have been handled with care and were pretty timid until recently. So I was fascinated to hear some plain speaking from the CEO of Cricket Australia (CA), James Sutherland, during an International Women's Day event in 2015. He was clear about the need for the sport to become accessible to women, both as fans and players. About a year later we met to discuss the progress towards the CA goal to make cricket a game for all Australians. It was a busy mid-afternoon and I noticed plenty of activity and an equal mix of men and women around the CA headquarters, just a few metres from the internationally renowned Melbourne Cricket Ground.

The goal was never going to be to create a separate 'women's cricket department', he says, but instead to normalise girls and women as fans or cricketers. And Australian women have played cricket in national competitions for over 80 years, he reminds me. While that might be true, few would suggest their participation was more than on the margins, and as an iconic Australian sport it has remained resolutely masculine until now. But Sutherland says that can change, and it is. Australians do consider themselves egalitarian in their thinking, and there's a commercial element to this direction. The more girls who grow up with a bat and ball in their hands, the more will grow up to be fans of the game and watch it. 'We had the right philosophy but until recent times haven't put the resource emphasis that we might. Our strategy is about how do we become more popular and [understand] why people are embracing cricket. We need to broaden our thinking around that and the obstacles to it.'

There's some pretty strong evidence women's cricket is grabbing public attention. The CBA-sponsored women's team already has lots of fans, the last three Twenty20 World Cup matches were well supported and the Women's Big Bash League really attracted attention with very high ratings, even outdoing the men's A League football during the same period.[5] So much for the popular idea that women's sport is boring because women are not strong or talented enough. In fact Sutherland says it was the women's matches that had a halo effect on the men's Big Bash and not the other way around. 'The real focus was to highlight the pathway and opportunities for girls and women to play cricket and that it's a sport for girls too. We want people to understand and question why are the girls not playing cricket? Maybe the father's mindset is one of the obstacles and we are trying to change that too.'

That has meant a grassroots effort to support cricket in schools for boys and girls. The number of girls playing at this early stage has increased significantly, but it has yet to translate into the club cricket system. The current pathway from women's school to State cricket looks a bit like the Eiffel Tower and the men's looks like a pyramid, he explains. That sounds a lot like the pathway for women into senior management jobs in most organisations. And the reaction so far to the moves to involve women in the game? Sutherland doesn't underestimate the impact of traditional mindsets but points out that unlike male-dominated workplaces such as the Defence Force, cricket is built on a volunteer base. There's a constant shift in that support base and the people who coach local teams every week. Sport makes a contribution to society as well, and has a strong community profile. 'We want our cricket community to represent our Australian society. And if you want to get a proposition across you have to get the fundamentals to change. One of the things the Women's Big Bash League does is put the games on a pedestal and it's on TV and in the newspaper. It pushes momentum.'

There's no reason to believe the goal of equally representing men and women at all levels of the game isn't achievable, Sutherland says, and something happened in the media coverage of women's sport during 2015. 'Where that came from I don't know, but I think there's a real wave that's coming through now and we would like to think we are at the front of that. But other sports have as well. The day that broadcasters start paying for the rights to broadcast women's cricket – that will be a sign of the value it is given. The aspiration is to have as many women's teams as men's teams at every level.'

While the goals for women's cricket are laudable, and audiences are building for the women's competition, there remains much to be done when it comes to better pay and conditions for professional players. Although a significant increase was announced in April 2016, doubling the total for female players to $4.23 million or about $100 000 annually for each team member, it still leaves them far behind the men, who can earn up to $2 million a year.[6] Revelations in late 2016 that women players were asked to sign a contract stating they were not pregnant showed significant challenges remain in closing the gap between rhetoric and reality if the sport is to be repositioned.

This gap will need to be addressed by Cricket Australia's leadership, along with countering assumptions held for more than a century about the mainstream popularity of and appetite for women's cricket. When women are fully recognised professionals and a major part of the audience, it will change who gets to make all kinds of decisions about the way the sport is organised and how it runs. It must also transform the fundamental power base of a sport that has been viewed by many as synonymous with parts of a traditional Australian masculine identity.

It was in the middle of researching this area of gender and sport that I read about research into women's teams in the international football arena. Since 2003, FIFA has ranked the women's national soccer teams of all member countries each year by performance and quality. In research conducted with Columbia's Ashley Martin and INSEAD's Pooja Mishra and

Roderick Swaab, consulting firm McKinsey found that the gender equality of a country predicts women's FIFA rankings even after controlling for population size and per capita GDP. When women have more power and opportunity in a country as a whole, that country's female soccer team has a competitive advantage.[7]

The chance for women to exercise more power in many workplaces remains limited, however, and while that much is clear from the statistics, the impact of this marginalisation on women's behaviour and confidence is less clear (more on this in chapter 8). Leaders like Parkinson are shifting their thinking to confront these covert elements too. Instead of assuming that women's lack of assertiveness, for example, is an outcome of their gender rather than the environment they work in, such leaders have begun to scrutinise closely the processes and the impact of stereotypes that can add up to discrimination.[8]

Senior Australian businessmen viewed women as less capable of problem solving than their male peers (even though their capacity and work outcomes were regarded as comparable).in research conducted in 2011 by Chief Executive Women and consulting firm Bain.[9] And there's a pattern here that is not just observable at the top levels or in professional ranks. The particular skills that women are deemed deficient in happen to be the exact ingredients crucial to more powerful, decision-making jobs. That is not a coincidence. There's plenty of entitlement and privilege being defended around those corner offices.

Surely then it would be fair to assume that most of the sexism and indeed the need to shift traditional norms could be sidestepped by just becoming your own boss? Small business is at the opposite end of the employment spectrum to a major government department or a high-profile sporting body, and it is a sector often thought of as a safe haven for women. But while it isn't usually described as male dominated, the sector has a surprising number of similar stumbling blocks for women, including in the entrepreneurial and startup space. This includes stereotypical ideas about the skills women are deemed to have, their appetite for risk, and the impact this can have on access to capital and networks.

Women do turn to small business because of problems they encounter with inflexibility (see chapter 2) and bias as employees. But it doesn't always work out as planned, because some of the gender attitudes and discrimination they face in workplaces can translate into the small business arena. And it can be much harder to lobby for change when you are a one-woman show.

Challenges to the gender status quo in the small business sector have slowly been gathering pace, with some entrepreneurs coming up with ways to address barriers and make building a business as accessible to women as men. A few years ago, Sydney businesswoman Yolanda Vega realised there was no dedicated resource for women in the small business sector within major sector bodies such as the Australian Chamber of Commerce and Industry (ACCI). So she started her own organisation: The Australian Women's Chamber of Commerce and Industry (AWCCI).

Instead of working from generic statistics, the AWCCI soon ran its own research on women in the sector and found the majority of female business operators – 93.3 per cent – were working in small business, while 78 per cent of respondents had left employment at middle to upper management level to start their businesses.[10] Research suggests that the number of women starting their own businesses has doubled since 2007, according to Vega, who has continued to lobby for greater attention to and data about women in the sector, including a breakdown of who is winning government contracts. Although the data revealed there were almost 1 million women trading in Australia, many of them were economically disadvantaged, with more than half being unable to pay themselves a wage.[11]

The growth in the number of Australian female business owners has nevertheless continued, but digging a little deeper into the statistics tells a different story. The 2015 labour force data shows women account for around a third, or 34 per cent, of business operators, according to the former minister for small business, Bruce Billson.[12] But while that trajectory has steadily climbed over the past 20 years, in line with other OECD (Organisation for Economic Co-operation and Development) countries, women remain 'substantially under-represented as entrepreneurs', according to OECD data.[13]

One evening in Sydney in 2014 I joined a group of women and men at the headquarters of the Commonwealth Bank for a regular 'Heads Over Heels' networking night. The event was designed to give women access to the same sorts of opportunities to build connections and get advice as many men find in the market. Janet Menzies, who was also program director for Male Champions of Change, co-founded and chaired Heads Over Heels (and was named one of the top 50 professionals working for diversity by *The Economist* in 2015) along with Melissa Winder and Dr Alex Birrell. The organisation helps female entrepreneurs grow business through connections to suppliers, partners and customers – many of them men. Luckily there is now a range of these organisations, including Springboard Enterprises and Scale Investors, which recognise that women have no particular lack of ability in setting up their businesses but need access to a system that is just as biased as the traditional hierarchies they have often fled.

That evening at Heads Over Heels, three female business founders explained how they had set up their businesses and the support they could most use to get to the next stage. One woman and her business partner had worked at a large IT company and struggled to get basic domestic chores organised (clearly this was seen as their responsibility at home) and so set up an online service for finding cleaners and household help. Another had established an online corporate events company using her lengthy experience in the sector. There was no sign of the much-cited lack of ambition or aversion to risk from these women but they did face challenges in accessing the same support networks as men. After their presentations, people formed groups or huddles, each with a mix of experienced finance, marketing and IT professionals who offered suggestions and connections to help.

Why do women need help to access this kind of expertise? There are some factors that are familiar to diversity practitioners in the corporate sector: the world of venture funding is dominated by men, and women tend to start smaller businesses than their male peers in sectors that may not appear attractive or high growth to such men. The CEO of US advertising tech start-up Vivoom, Katherine Hays, believes male venture capitalists are happy enough to give female entrepreneurs capital for 'girl stuff', such as online clothing or make-up sites, but when it comes to hard-core technology there's less interest.[14]

More research backs this up. A report from early stage investment firm Female Founders Fund in the US found that out of about 200 Bay Area startups in 2015 that received series A funding – defined as a financing round of between US$3 million and $15 million – only 8 per cent were led by women, a decline of nearly 30 per cent from the previous year. The record for New York companies founded by women that received series A funding in 2015 was only a little better at 13 per cent, the same as 2014, according to the study. The 2015 Startup Muster survey found that 'the Australian startup community still has a stark gender gap, with only 24 per cent of companies founded by women, up from 19 per cent in 2013'.[15] And the reason? 'Biases absolutely play a part' in the funding disparity, said Laura Huang, a professor of management at Wharton Business School. 'In the context of entrepreneurship, there is so little objective data to go on in the early stages of a venture [that it] makes it easier [for VCs] to be influenced, whether implicitly or explicitly, and make judgments based on personal attributes like gender.'[16] On top of that, people tend to feel more comfortable with others who look and sound a lot like them, making it harder for women to break through when men dominate in the sector. No amount of assertiveness training for female business owners will open a firmly closed door to those crucial networks.

This clearly does not deter women from setting up small businesses, as we have seen, but their motivation also reflects some depressing realities about rigid workplaces where the shift in thinking about gender and jobs has definitely not begun. The first big study of maternal self-employment in Australia suggests that it is an option of last resort for many women and carries serious long-term economic consequences, according to

Dr Meraiah Foley. She surveyed and interviewed 60 self-employed Australian mothers about why they started their own businesses instead of staying with their previous employers or seeking new jobs.[17] Inhospitable workplace cultures and the high cost of childcare were the two main factors.

These findings are a reminder that the action from the men turning up at Heads Over Heels, and by leaders like Martin Parkinson, James Sutherland, Lance Hockridge – along with Gordon Cairns, the chair of Woolworths, which reached 50 per cent women on its board in 2016 – are still the exceptions and a long way from being the rule. But long-term transformations have to start somewhere. And their advocacy and work on gender barriers has the potential to make an impact, from the biggest end of business to the smallest sole trader, because they don't fix women but enlist men in reframing and legitimising different rules and attitudes.

One of those basic conditions has long been strongly associated with women and therefore earned a bad reputation for those on the fast track to management or keen to be seen as serious workers: flexibility. It is often featured as a cornerstone of diversity programs, and the entire area has attracted attention as the rhetoric moves from maternity leave to normalising different ways of working. It's a hard slog to stop viewing flexible work through the prism of fixing women and to start getting men on board and involved as advocates. There are some important lessons to be learned from these efforts, covered in the next chapter. But legitimising these options in some organisations also motivates some men to examine the way they want to work and care. And it helps to redefine flexibility, from being seen as a compliance-driven distraction for women to a necessity for many dual-income couples and younger men who have a very different view of parenting to their fathers'. That's an almighty struggle which could have massive repercussions.

CHAPTER 2

The fight for flexibility

'Why, after all these decades of campaign, reform, research and thought about how we can best get women into the workplace, are we so slow to pick up that the most important next step is how to get men out of it?'

ANNABEL CRABB, *THE WIFE DROUGHT*

IT'S A PERFECT SYDNEY SUMMER morning and a large business audience has gathered at the iconic Opera House to hear about new research on flexibility in the workplace. The study, commissioned by Chief Executive Women (CEW) and consulting firm Bain, shows women are still far more likely to work part-time in Australia, and men who decide to take the flexibility track face a wall of disapproval and career penalties too.

The presentation of the findings is followed by a discussion, and a business-suited man puts up his hand. He explains he has taken four months' leave to care for his lively 15-month-old son. The biggest revelation for him has been the strong expectations of what men and women might do during what he calls the 'years of disruption'. Workplaces, particularly the professional services environment he works in, are not adjusting to flexibility but instead changing the job status of those who take the flexible options, such as him and his wife.

'We have friends whose careers have stalled because they have been moved out of client-facing roles. It hasn't happened to me', he explains, 'because my employers think it's temporary and I'd get my career back on track. I call this mutual career sabotage, but once it [flexibility] is the norm, you can't afford to move everyone out of the high-profile roles because there would be no-one to do them'.

The audience applauds his comments, which are a useful addition to the conversation. But the woman I am sitting with (who is head of diversity for a large listed company) points out that none of the women, who already raised equally pertinent points about the struggle to break down narrow thinking on flexibility, were applauded. Clearly it is still a novelty to hear about a man taking these options and even rarer for him to speak out at this kind of forum. While women are expected to do the caring work, men can often find they are given kudos for doing anything in this arena – although as the report points out, not if they formally work flexibly and mess up the usual narrative about who should do the caring. That is a step too far in upending stereotypes, even though the case for improved access to flexible work is getting stronger in many parts of the world.

As the research points out, the demand for flexibility is higher than ever and not only from women. Demographic data in Australia reveals that 'the percentage of dual-income households in Australia has increased from 40% in 1983 to nearly 60% in 2013. We have seen the percentage of working mothers with children under the age of 18 increase by 6% in the past decade. The aging population means employees are staying in the workplace longer, often in a more flexible capacity. And the current generation of new recruits, known as millennials, has very different work expectations than their baby boomer parents. Survey after survey has shown what millennials want most is to work flexibly.'[1]

While flexibility can clearly mean many different things to different cohorts, there is still a tendency to equate it with part-time work for mothers. And indeed more than two in five (43 per cent) of Australia's working women are part-time, compared with 14 per cent of men.[2] The problem is there is still far more talk than action: 'flexible working is still viewed as the exception to the rule in the majority of Australian companies. Fewer than 50 per cent of organisations have a workplace flexibility policy. And even when such policies exist, they are not always effectively utilised.'[3]

Interestingly, most of the ensuing discussion of the research at the Opera House wasn't about the need to get women to adjust to workplace norms but almost the other way around – for the norms about when, how and where work is done to be pulled out of the 'pink ghetto' of remedial measures for mums and into the mainstream. This is in fact a family issue, said Diane Smith-Gander, CEW president at the time. But the few men who have tried to work flexibly – from home, or varying start/finish

times for example – are also battling the legacy of this remedial approach to fit women into a traditional male breadwinner
model.

This effort has been spectacularly unsuccessful. Women who
take flexibility options have usually been harshly penalised for
not fitting the usual workplace pattern: lack of progression and
pay, poor attachment to the workforce and as a result, a chronic
lack of superannuation. And that's if they even have the luxury
of being able to work less, because a lot of women in casualised
jobs would love more regular work and predictable shifts. It's the
case of too much flexibility for low-income earners and too little
for more educated professionals.

Despite the applause for the young man at the research
launch, when it comes to flexibility, the results show that men
who take up these options are not getting much support on the
job from their work peers. They also suffer from career penalties,
just like many women who have been consigned to the 'mummy
track' or have even found their job has disappeared altogether
after a 'restructure'. Men interviewed for the Bain/CEW study
who were 'not satisfied with their flexible working experiences'
cite a lack of senior support and the negative view their peers
and management hold of working flexibly as key issues.

'While opportunities exist, the environment that management creates makes it difficult to participate', said one.
Underscoring the cultural challenge, 'the arrangements worked
as agreed, but I have felt judgment for using them', said another.
In addition, the impact on career progression is stark: 'My boss
told me I wouldn't be able to get promoted working part-time',
said another respondent.[4] These men haven't been able to eradicate the stigma of flexibility – the association with mothers is

so strong they are being penalised for not only being less serious about their work, but for behaving in a way that is incongruous with masculinity.

The male breadwinner model has a lot to answer for in this arena. Not all men view flexibility as a desirable notion and some have a strong attachment to the competitive, chest-thumping model that sees notching up the longest hours in the office as a worthwhile goal. In fact this syndrome has been dubbed 'conspicuous work' by researchers at Maastricht University, who found a correlation between happiness and men (not women) working more hours than their friends and colleagues.[5] This was regardless of their working schedules or income. Go figure.

And while men may take a hit for working flexibly, it's unlikely they will suffer all the long-term motherhood penalties that women face in their working lives, such as less pay. The stigma of flexibility does apply to men but once again being a woman brings extra and enduring problems. Men, meanwhile, may get a happiness boost from outworking their friends and colleagues, but they are also able to do so when there's someone at home to feed the kids, or do the shopping. Even leaving childcare out of the equation, the data clearly shows women are still doing the lion's share of housework, no matter what their income. In Australian homes with a male breadwinner, women do an average of 27.6 hours of housework and men 14.5 hours, according to 2014 findings.[6] But the kicker is that when women earn more than their male partners they still do 21.5 hours of chores per week, and men 17.5 hours.

Fortunately, more and more men are finding social norms have changed when it comes to childcare and parenting these days, particularly when their partners are in paid work too.

Which is just as well because there are very few first-time parents of either gender who aren't side-swiped by the sheer tumultuous upheaval of babies and their awkward refusal to fit into schedules. Unfortunately, I've discovered most children don't grow out of this stubborn failure to do what their parents would like, but you do get used to it. And to the guilt that seems to linger around motherhood. A friend once told a group of us, all mothers, that her mum would routinely and rather abruptly turn to her when she was growing up and ask if she 'was having a happy childhood?' Her surprised daughter usually agreed because she didn't know what else to say. And while those of us listening to this anecdote laughed in surprise at the blatant neediness of the question, I think we all sort of understood it too. Mothers don't know if they are doing the right thing but they do know who will get blamed if it all goes wrong.

In no surprise to many mums, it turns out reproduction and the average workplace regime are a very poor fit, as are the demands of elderly, frail and demented parents. Sadly, I again speak from experience. But the messy reality of gestation, birth, nurturing and aged care has long been framed as not just the domain of women but a significant disruption to the wheels of commerce (or government, the health system etc.), which they should primarily cope with or bear the consequences. There's more than a touch of biological determinism in this view and many of the more insidious parts of the gender deficit model tend to reinforce the idea that women are to blame for having been cursed with too much natural caring concern and too little killer instinct. It's a no-win situation, really, particularly for powerful women who don't have children, such as former Australian prime minister Julia Gillard, who couldn't win a trick on this front. She was castigated for not having kids but instead of picking up brownie points for extra dedication to the job, Gillard was often painted as cold and calculating. Men without children, such as former NSW premier Bob Carr, rarely face as much rancour for failing to reproduce.

The stories we hear repeatedly about the formidable barriers women face with jobs because of their natural disadvantage as childbearers reinforce a range of other ideas about their deficits in areas such as ambition. And it has a fascinating legacy. Who hasn't heard about the 'biological clock' and thought it was just a reflection of medical fact? But while fertility does decrease with age, the idea of the ticking time bomb is largely a construct which became popular – surprise, surprise – about the time more women were entering the professions in the 1980s, according to US author Moira Weigel's essay 'The foul reign of the biological clock'. Just as women gained access to education and birth control, enabling them to make bolder decisions about their lives and reproduction, a great big finger-wagging threat to greedy career types materialised in the media. Missing out on having a baby and fulfilling a 'biological destiny' was neatly played off against success in the workplace. The clock wasn't just about awareness of fertility – it was a reaction to the effects of women's liberation.

'First, conversations about the "biological clock" pushed women towards motherhood, suggesting that even if some of the gendered double standards about sex were eroding, there would always be this difference: women had to plan their love lives with an eye to having children before it was "too late". Second, the metaphor suggested that it was only natural that women who tried to compete with men professionally, and to become mothers as well, would do so at a disadvantage. The idea that being female is a weakness is embedded in the origin of the phrase "biological clock"', she found.[7]

This wretched ticking bomb metaphor also exaggerates the differences between the genders in a pseudo-scientific and mostly negative way for women in the workplace. By bringing it up repeatedly over the decades since it was coined, the impending fertility deadline has come to be seen as a women's personal and professional responsibility that needs to be dealt with individually, rather than by changing the rules of work and care to allow for reproduction. Sadly, although understandably given its pervasiveness, this idea of where the problem lies has been absorbed by women, who have taken the blame on themselves and 'listened to experts who told them what experts always tell women: There is something terribly wrong with you! But luckily, there is also something new and expensive that you can buy to fix it'.[8] Little wonder consulting packages and books of remedial tips for women who try to combine family and a job have thrived, while more unsettling options to make adjustments to workplace norms and rules have been ignored or seen as unnecessary and unfair.

Equating childbearing with a personal and inconvenient affliction reinforces the idea that women are naturally ill-suited to paid jobs, much less management. And it's helped keep workplace flexibility discussions about policy and practice on the women's agenda. That usually means it's been marginalised. Even in countries where there is some form of paid parenting leave and subsidised childcare, such as Australia, it's frightening how often the cost of children is seen as hitting the mother's hip pocket, with barely a mention of a partner's income. Discussions and events about flexibility are usually full of women because, well, women give birth and lactate, don't they? And yet, addressing these clashes, which are only set to increase, along with the number of working couples, can only happen if there is a broader debate that includes men, and a serious look at mainstreaming some different ways and hours of working. This is actually not a difficult intellectual feat (as we shall see). Many employees already do some work from home, vary their hours or use annual leave variations. Decoupling the flexibility debate from women is a first step.

And while there's no question men are increasingly supporting flexibility in theory, beware the wolf in feminist clothing. It's remarkable how often I've heard senior men waxing lyrical about the benefits of flexible work, only to find on closer examination that they have never had any practical experience of anything approaching flexibility – quite the reverse, usually. Most of them are locked into an extreme worker model and when they do make the occasional exception – for a child's swimming carnival, for example – that's exactly what it is: an exception. And when you are CEO, and take some time out once in a blue moon, of course it's unlikely you will be penalised for a perceived lack of serious intention in your workplace. More likely you will be lauded. So while it's great to hear the positive rhetoric from male leaders, it does need to be matched by genuine role modelling at all levels of organisations or flexibility will only remain an option for women with small children.

Not long before I was due to finish this book, Male Champions of Change asked me to interview a number of executives who were working flexibly, to publish as a list of senior role models. One candidate was the CEO of Network Ten, Paul

Anderson, who confessed he had been the 'first in the office, last to leave' type for years. These days he sees things differently and tries to model flexibility by working from home once a week, and varying his hours to make time for his family and cycling. But he admits it's a bit different for the CEO. 'It's easier for me to do it because I don't suffer from the same level of scrutiny and I think it [more acceptance] comes from a culture thing.' He's seeing more examples of flexible routines emerging from the ranks below, although there's also been scepticism about whether he is really practising what he preaches: 'People say, "Is he really not coming in on Thursday morning?"', he said.

Australian managers' need to keep their eye on employees is particularly acute compared to other countries, according to Associate Professor Rae Cooper from Sydney University Business School, an expert in the area of women and work. And flexibility for those on the career ladder is tricky. 'I think it's particularly hard in middle management to practise flexibility; these people often find they are trapped in long hours working and while there may be lots of talk about flexible hours they get bigger and bigger jobs and they have more and more people looking at them. I actually think it's easier for people at the pinnacle of management to enact flexibility than it is for mid-managers.'

In some places the scrutiny from peers is a real inhibitor to flexibility – partnerships in particular come to mind. There are signs of change emerging, however, even in those bastions of time-sheets and all-nighters – the top-tier law firms. In early 2015 I got a call from a female barrister who was active in the Women Lawyers Association of NSW. One of her tasks was to look at flexibility, and she thought a panel discussion aimed at men seemed a better step than another forum for women. I was asked to help arrange the panel and line up some speakers. I have interviewed lots of people about workplace flexibility over the years and one of the most compelling thinkers and consultants in the area is Dr Graeme Russell, who co-chairs the Diversity Council of Australia's research committee. He joined me for the event, which was held at one of the top-tier law firms in Australia, Allens, late in 2015.

Russell kicked off in fine style by saying that in his experience, not one organisation in Australia has really grasped and applied true flexibility. Despite the increasing need for change, and the technology to enable it, progress was slow, he explained, and that included at organisations that were sponsoring research into new ways of working and job redesign. Many were still struggling with the broader concept of flexibility. A few months before the panel, Russell and I had discussed the same topic for an article on law firms and flexibility for a legal journal. He told me it's often a very difficult conversation with people because they don't get the scale of the topic, which is about reframing the way we work and careers. The conversation usually defaults to women, he said. 'There are two elements that I think are key to change: the career factor – what's accepted and how do you get to where you need to be; and job and work design.'

Shifting the traditional way work gets done and what gets rewarded over the longer term is part of the process. But it often ends up being a discussion about women making relatively short-term adjustments to hours during childbearing and rearing years. As long as this is the case, it will be designated a special initiative, which means it gets some energy and attention periodically but then rapidly loses momentum, he added. It's time to really get serious about this topic as demand grows across all age and gender brackets. 'Let's have an open discussion about work and that's going to lead to productivity and performance and to flexible work, because it's an enabler for change to happen and [delivers] more effective and productive workplaces. It can be done.'

I've always disliked the use of the word 'balance' in this discussion, because I don't know anyone who is balanced and certainly not when they are trying to hold down a job and care for small children. Or aged parents. But I do want to use the word in this context – that the debate on how to prepare for the new world of work is about shifting the balance of responsibility for managing this complex equation from the shoulders of women (along with the blame when it doesn't pan out) and to make workplaces mould more closely to the needs of their employees. Flexibility and parenting leave are still too firmly linked and too often seen as disruptive and a deterrent to hiring even young women, despite the rhetoric. Maternity discrimination was experienced by nearly half of Australian women in employment surveyed in Australia,[9] and a staggering 75 per cent of pregnant women or new mothers surveyed in the UK reported facing discrimination in 2016.[10]

Despite Russell's finding that most companies still hadn't fully grasped flexibility, there are some encouraging signs of change. One of the more familiar examples is Telstra's All Roles Flex program, which allows any employee to ask for flexibility in their job. The effects have been closely monitored by diversity head, Troy Roderick (and details published in early 2016 in the Bain/CEW study). Following its introduction, 84 per cent of Telstra employees agreed that they were able to access the flexibility they need to balance their work and personal lives, up by 4 per cent from 2013. Other results tracked by Telstra include:

- Female representation among commencements is at 42.9 per cent in 2015, up from 36.7 per cent for the same period last year;
- The number of women joining Telstra exceeds the number of women leaving for the eighth successive quarter, ending a retention issue that had persisted for some time;
- Accompanying Telstra's high rates of parental leave return and retention (higher than 90 per cent), the number of male managers at Telstra taking primary parental leave increased in the past year from 0.8 per cent to 2.3 per cent.[11]

When Telstra's program was first discussed in 2014, the cynics were quick to dismiss it as 'gender washing' that was unlikely to have much effect, but the results indicate there has been a shift. The number of men accessing flexibility is still very low, however, suggesting more work is needed to challenge assumptions about the ideal worker. One of the fears – that the new policy would open up a floodgate of demands for part-time work – has proved to be largely unfounded, although that may be due to the continuing stigma part-time work carries. Professional services firm PwC and bank ANZ have both announced similar policies since the Telstra launch. The trick will now be ensuring that the policy is put into practice and actually encourages more men to take it up – progress on this front has been slow.

At ANZ, the head of HR, Susie Babani, acknowledged there has been rhetoric and policy but not too much practice in this area.[12] 'We've had policies on flexible working for a number of years but usage was sporadic and very much depended on a

'Leadership Lottery' – if you had a leader who "got it" then flex was just part of the day-to-day norms and no big deal. But if you moved somewhere else or inherited a leader who didn't "get it", then working for the same company could feel very different indeed.' Part of ANZ's aim in making all roles flexible is tackling 'the misconceptions around "presenteeism", [such as] "flex employees lack commitment", "it's all too hard" and "this is only for junior people",' she said.

In 2016 another professional services firm, Grant Thornton, announced that workforce demographics and employee demand had been the drivers for new flexible options: after two years, employees can now access an extra week's leave through early access to long service leave (usually only available after 10 years); a more generous paid parental leave scheme and flexibility was also offered to all employees.

Caltex has also introduced options to improve the retention of women after childbearing. All primary carers who work for Caltex receive a 3 per cent bonus each quarter after returning from leave. The policy has been in place for several years to help offset the costs of childcare for parents. The company reported a 25 per cent increase in the number of women returning to work between 2013 and 2015 and an increased retention rate, which covers the cost of the extra pay.[13]

Aurizon, meanwhile, has taken another tack. In early 2016 the transport company announced a 'Shared Care' program, which offers 'half-pay' for a partner to take leave to care for a child in their first year, allowing the other partner to return to work full-time. The innovative program means a female employee at Aurizon who returns to full-time work in the first year after her child is born and whose partner has taken on full-time care of their child in that period (and takes leave without pay from their employer to do so) will receive 150 per cent of her salary, also up to a maximum of 26 weeks. When it was announced, the CEO at the time, Lance Hockridge, said Aurizon was taking a deliberately interventionist approach in its bid to build a more diverse and inclusive workforce. Although the announcement caused some raised eyebrows about the cost, Donna McMahon, vice president of HR Organisational Capability at Aurizon, told me the projections indicated the cost amounted to less than 0.2 per cent of overall expenditure. While the policy was in its infancy when we talked in mid-2016, McMahon said there were already several employees using it, and retention rates of women returning from leave (admittedly a very small group) were high: 94 out of 98 returned to their jobs in 2015.

Despite a persistent feeling that flexibility is completely at odds with a core military mandate – the ADF is technically on call to be mobilised within 24 hours – the case for change is gathering momentum in the Australian Defence Force. Flexible employment has been shown to enhance productivity and output, and the idea that part-time work is only one version is beginning to be more broadly understood. Other options include variable working hours, compressed working hours, working from home, working in another geographic location, job-sharing and flexible crewing/shifts. Not all ADF workplaces can accommodate flexible working arrangements, but commanders are being asked to consider improved flexibility where possible, according to a major study into flexible work in the ADF.[14]

Former army chief David Morrison introduced a measure where employees identified as the 'talent of the future' were guaranteed that after a period of absence they could return and would not lose seniority. It was a world first, and as a consequence women returning from maternity leave are now at an all-time high for the army. But negative stereotypes still linger. A key message to counter this is reinforcing the link between less rigid ways of working and improved retention of members, which in turn reduces spending on training and recruitment. Again, the focus is on matching ADF norms with community and business standards, and emphasising that flexibility will enhance, not reduce, capability.

Along with these welcome changes to policy, there's another argument that needs to be broadcast about flexibility in many businesses too. Until very recently, flexibility hasn't been seen as viable for any reason other than looking after small children (although elder care is starting to be mentioned too). But as Grant Thornton carefully put it, these measures are also about attracting and retaining a cohort of workers who want to have different working lives from their parents'. And of course, it's not only about kids or indeed caring responsibilities. Sometimes flexibility is about having the control and latitude to include other work, education or interests in your life. Having left a national law firm to start her own business, Sibenco Legal & Advisory, lawyer Susan Bennett told me her motivation was less about cutting back hours and more about having a sustainable and flexible career over the next few years when we spoke in 2014 for an article I was writing. Running her own firm has allowed Bennett to take on a bigger role in a family business, Ashgrove Cheese, in Tasmania.

Flexibility in workplaces is not the tall order it is often made out to be. No-one works 24 hours a day for seven days a week and 365 days a year. We all work flexibly to some degree, but pressure to be present has been on the increase in recent times. Despite access to technology making it possible to work from just about anywhere for at least some of the time, and to have output monitored too, there's an obsession with long hours in offices under the eye of managers. How odd to think that some of the most extreme worker examples come from the tech sector, which is on the cutting edge of mobile and virtual communications. Who knew even those innovators (and their bosses) at the cusp of the next new thing could be so staid about how and where they work?

But while it's feasible, whether in Silicon Valley or the local cafe, for flexibility to be successful, it has to be tackled on two levels: the practical, which is about educating and supporting employees who use it and the supervisors who manage it; and the intellectual, so that thinking shifts and it's not just seen as plugging a hole for mothers, complete with long-term job penalties.

Given these realities, organisations need to ensure that flexible arrangements work successfully for both men and women, the CEW/Bain report concludes. That's a step that requires so much more than normalising part-time hours, for example. It requires confronting the view that flexibility is essentially a remedial and temporary set of conditions designed for mums with low ambitions and narrow job horizons. And tackling the idea that it's a 'choice', complete with guilt and exhaustion, which women have only themselves to blame for making. It will also need to refocus this debate on the barriers to flexibility, such as adherence to the male breadwinner model and the bravado factor when long hours become a symbol of winning a competition with peers. In fact, it means recalibrating some pretty fundamental gender stereotypes.

Equating care work with low value and status is deeply embedded in our society. As former Sex Discrimination Commissioner Elizabeth Broderick often points out, Australians still hang on to the belief that a serious worker can throw every hour of the day at the job and a good mother stays at home with her children. These social standards mean approaches to flexibility have usually hinged on defining it as an aberration from the norm granted by special permission, which is ideally temporary and then carries well-deserved long-term career penalties.

Flexibility still sits very uneasily with current work mores, and of course the ultimate flexibility is when you have highly casualised workforces for low-skilled employees who don't even know if they will get a shift at all – the so-called zero hour contract. This is a savage and brutal system that particularly penalises parents, who are unable to access regular care or hold down a job if they can't cope with the unpredictable demands of employers. In this context, the kind of flexibility options large employers are offering is a nirvana indeed.

Even when employees have access to permanent flexibility, there continues to be a very traditional view of who should do the primary caring and the primary breadwinning. US author Anne-Marie Slaughter analysed this conflict in her book *Unfinished business*, and I got a chance to have a chat with and hear her speak at the All About Women conference at the Sydney Opera House in early 2016. She said it took her a long time to think through the ideas about the competing values of care and competition and how gendered these realms are in our society.

Later she told a packed audience about the way these two areas are so differently valued and why this mismatch remains the unfinished business of gender equality. Focusing on care creates a more inclusive feminism, she explained, and looking at competition reveals we have far too many men at the top and too many women at the bottom.

As she spoke about this dichotomy it became clear there were many implications for any future attempts at genuine flexibility in business. Many of them are about men, rather than fixing women. Men should be expected to be much more than helpers at home and become actual co-carers, and their gender roles need to be challenged just as women's have, she said. The way to start is changing assumptions and language: don't ask people what they do, call men working fathers, ask young men how they will fit work and family together, stop talking about a lead parent. Employers, too, should stop framing this as a women's issue but look at how we can work more productively when we have caring responsibilities. It's time, said Slaughter, to build an infrastructure of care in the same way you build an infrastructure for a thriving economy.

There's been lots of discussion in the business world in recent years about the future of work: how long we will all be working, the nature of jobs and the multiple careers we'll all have, as well as the mantra of innovation, mobility and agility in the new economy. The predictions that we will all live and work for much longer have made the flexibility debate very timely, as London Business School academic Lynda Gratton told me in mid-2016. Her book, *The 100-year life*, about the impact of longer lifespans, maps the social trends in the last two decades which have challenged norms around the 'standard' working week, the separation of work and leisure, and gender roles.[15] Access to education and the workplace for women has increased so there are more dual-income couples; childbearing is often planned and takes place later in life than just a few decades ago; technology has changed how and where work is done. These forces will significantly strengthen change in these areas, just as the Industrial Revolution did a century or so ago.[16]

While Gratton acknowledges there is currently a 'flexibility stigma' for both genders, this could change in the future if career breaks for men and women are the norm, and could lead to greater pay equity. But perhaps more significant is the potential for work to be restructured so that the current flexibility cost to employee or employer is reduced. 'If both men and women prefer more flexible working patterns then the nature of work is likely to be radically redesigned.'[17] As we chatted in the London Business School, Gratton explained that working lives in the future will be spread over much longer periods and see more of the dual-career couple, and a see-saw between paid and unpaid work for both genders. And the pattern we now associate with women – moving in and out of different kinds of work and flexibility – is more likely to be the norm and not the exception.

At the moment, women's paid working lives often extend unevenly over many decades, but are still defined by perceptions about a relatively short part of their lives spent in reproduction or in a caring role because of structural failure to make flexibility a norm. Normalising different models of work through programs such as All Roles Flex are a small but important step in changing this system. But these welcome moves can't work on their own to shift an array of damaging negative stereotypes about gender, ambition, skills and capacity, as we will see in the next chapters. Long before many women get to the point of needing or wanting parenting flexibility, they are struggling for a fair go in both getting and retaining a job.

CHAPTER 3

Who gets the job?

'It's important to realise that men have been subtly advantaged throughout their career and women need support.'

STEPHEN FITZGERALD, DIRECTOR, MALE CHAMPION OF CHANGE; FORMER CEO, GOLDMAN SACHS AUSTRALIA

THE GRAFFITI WAS HARD TO avoid: 'Diversity = Less jobs for men' was daubed along the side of a rail carriage owned by transport company Aurizon in 2015. CEO at the time Lance Hockridge said he wasn't surprised by the message, and although he doesn't know for sure who did it, there's a pretty fair chance it was an aggrieved male worker. After all, Hockridge had been pretty clear and decisive about his plans to get more women and indigenous workers into the male-dominated company and obviously not everyone was happy with this direction. Not that he was deterred.

'The graffiti on the train is true – diversity does mean fewer jobs for men and shows the feeling on the cultural change process', he told me in early 2016 as we discussed the diversity work at the company. Intervention to change traditional practices meant a close look at recruitment from entry level up to the top. 'We recruited eight apprentices in a recent intake at one of our sites and we set ourselves a goal of 100 per cent women. On the back of that graffiti there was speculation about how feasible this was and whether we'd get the best apprentices. Not only did we get 100 per cent women, their supervisors have said they are highly capable and their presence is helping change the workplace culture.'

There's been a gradual understanding at the company that this is not change for the sake of it but essential for future growth. Anecdotally, Hockridge believes the attitudes of a sceptical group were shifting because the more dire predictions and concerns tend to dissipate as norms were altered. 'It's a light-bulb moment that this is not so bad after all', he told me over coffee in early 2016. His work has gained plenty of accolades and not just in Australia, where he is a Male Champion of Change and a member of the Defence Force Gender Equality Advisory Board. Just before we met he became the first Australian to win an award for leadership at the UN Women's Empowerment Principles annual event for his demonstrated commitment to and implementation of policies that advance and empower women in the workplace, marketplace and community.

Back in Australia, Hockridge has become an unlikely disrupter in the gender and work space. An unassuming and quietly spoken man, he can certainly, however, make people listen. You could have heard a pin drop at a panel discussion in Sydney in 2014 when Hockridge talked about one of the changes he introduced to the recruitment process for the company. When Aurizon was filling a role with a candidate from outside the company, and there was a choice between a male and female candidate with similar skills, the woman would get the job, he said. It's what we used to call affirmative action: steps taken to favour marginalised groups so they were given the same opportunities as everyone else. Although some in the audience believed it was very difficult to see any two candidates for a job as equally capable, and the aim should always be to put the best person in the job, this recruitment strategy was partly motivated by a need to start examining the subjective assumptions about exactly what makes someone the 'best' candidate and why.

To some of those listening that evening in Sydney, the recruitment policy sounded very much like the blatant unfairness that such measures actually set out to change. But, importantly, Hockridge said action in this area was a business priority, particularly in the competitive listed company space where Aurizon needs to attract skilled employees in a very tight labour market. The aim is to proactively boost the current level of female employees from about 16 per cent to 30 per cent. And Hockridge has a very clear attitude about the need to change the gender ratio.

'It's not a women's issue, it's a leadership issue', he told the forum. 'If it's not the blokes that make the change, it's not going to happen. It requires positive intervention and that is the journey we've taken, particularly in a post-privatisation world. Unless you do things that are making the organisation uncomfortable, we are not making progress. The predominant approach has been exactly the reverse. You can't just have the preconditions and expect it will happen naturally.'

It's refreshing to hear the word 'intervention' used in a discussion about dismantling the barriers women face to being recruited or promoted. There's been plenty of heat and little light in recent years, and the onus is usually on women to do the shaping up or shipping out. Like a broken record, the old excuses are circulated that the problems are self-inflicted. Women don't put their hands up for a job, they lack confidence and (foolishly, it is implied) feel they need to have most of the skills listed for a role before they will apply. They 'lean out' instead of in. And so it goes on.

The idea that women are particularly anxious about having 80 per cent or so of job requirements before putting their hat in the ring has taken on the status of a truism, and I've been told by very senior men in the business world that it is 'a fact'. Except it actually isn't. This piece of urban myth is often said to be based on the results of a Hewlett Packard (HP) study that tested the idea. But apparently no such study exists and there has never been strong empirical evidence that such a gender split between male and female job seekers occurs. A concerted effort to establish whether there was a study done at HP found no evidence for it but many people refer to it, including Sheryl Sandberg in her book *Lean In*.[1] A much more likely reading would be that some people are more likely to apply with fewer credentials than others. Gender probably isn't the only issue here, but it does tie in nicely with how we think women are likely to behave. So of course it is repeated, with much head nodding from men and women, because it confirms stereotype-enforcing hearsay.

Meanwhile, the assumption that appointing or promoting a woman to a role – particularly if the decision-maker is a woman – occurs in a vacuum, separate from social and workplace norms and attitudes, and therefore has a neutral impact on those who make the decision, turns out to be wide of the mark too. Actually, looking at what happens when women and non-white executives support other women and minority groups shows there are serious repercussions for those people, according to researchers.[2] One study by US business school academics Stephanie Johnson and David Hekman surveyed 350 executives on several diversity-valuing behaviours, such as whether they respected cultural, religious, gender and racial differences, valued working with a diverse group of people, and felt comfortable managing people from different racial or cultural backgrounds.

'Much to our surprise, we found that engaging in diversity-valuing behaviors did not benefit any of the executives in terms of how their bosses rated their competence or performance [...] Even more striking, we found that women and non-white executives who were reported as frequently engaging in these behaviors were rated much *worse* by their bosses, in terms of competence and performance ratings, than their female and non-white counterparts who did not actively promote balance. For all the talk about how important diversity is within organizations, white and male executives aren't rewarded, career-wise, for engaging in diversity-valuing behavior, and nonwhite and female executives actually get punished for it.'

So supporting diversity in your job isn't a successful career tactic. But the findings get worse. When it comes to those crucial calls on who gets the job or the promotion, much the same dynamic occurs. Participants in the study were asked to assess a recruiting decision by a series of fictitious managers of different gender, race and age groups. 'Participants rated non-white managers and female managers as less effective when they hired a non-white or female job candidate instead of a white male candidate [...] Basically, all managers were judged harshly if they hired someone who looked like them, unless they were a white male.'

The results reveal that in most workplaces, white men remain the default when suitability and competence are considered, and have some latitude to deviate from the rules, because they are members of the high-status or power group. But when women or ethnic minorities make these decisions, their competence is not assumed and their marginalised status triggers a stereotype of incompetence, which is then punished. (By the way, these findings also provide a useful resource for countering the exasperated cry of 'Why don't you demand a job/raise/fair go?' that entitled men sometimes direct to women when this topic comes up. Now we can see why. When women ask or, heaven forbid, demand these status enhancers they can be penalised. That's why.)

The researchers concluded that their study 'highlights the importance of putting appropriate structures and processes in place to guarantee the fair evaluation of women and minorities. The challenge of creating equality should not be placed on the shoulders of individuals who are at greater risk of being crushed by the weight of this goal.' Having been involved in quite a lot of recruiting processes and hiring decisions over the years, I wasn't surprised to read that decisions made by women can rebound on them but less so on men. Many women know this dynamic exists and are constrained by it, which of course doesn't help change the diversity mix.

Fair evaluation of female employees is certainly not a given in all organisations. Performance feedback for women, numerous studies have found, is often stuck in a deficit model, focusing on their manner and how they communicate, which leads to negative ratings. Vague feedback is more often given to women, according to US research by the Clayman Institute, which analysed the language of 200 redacted performance reviews from a high-tech company.[3] Women received about half as much feedback linked to business outcomes as men, and were 3.2 times more likely to receive feedback about having a negative (aggressive) communication style as men. In many cases, the research found, these comments show that women were being criticised for behaviour that might be considered leader-like if it came from a man. Expressions like 'executive presence' are used to define leadership but are difficult to pin down and highly subjective, said the Clayman Institute's Lori Mackenzie, who suggests banning it altogether. She also suggests using clear skills-based criteria in performance reviews and blocking undue criticism of women's communication styles to help change the dynamics.

That seems sensible. So does avoiding asking the victims of bias to fix it up themselves when they are the ones who will get penalised for doing just that. Telling women en masse they have to pull their socks up to get a job has been a hugely counterproductive exercise. It assumes all factors and decisions are viewed equally and neutrally in the workforce – which is clearly not the case – that there are transparent and clear definitions of 'merit' (more on this shortly) and that women are prone to sabotage their chances because of inbuilt deficiencies. By droning on and on about how women just need to 'man up' and put their hands up or face the consequences is about as sensible as telling the victims of violent crime that they brought it on themselves.

It also rather presumes that most women have never tried the 'masculine', direct approach, because if they had then it would have worked out for many of them. Actually, we don't know for certain if a reasonable number of women start out with plenty of chutzpah when it comes to getting a job but find themselves beaten down by the process and the bias over time. But studies of ambition levels in women would suggest this could be so, with levels similar for men and women until about ten years into the workforce, when women record less ambition. And other research, including a massive study of Harvard Business School alumni, found women had the same ambition levels and career aspirations as men and did not routinely 'opt out' of their paid jobs to care for family full-time.[4] And those who had left paid work mostly did so not because of a persistent tug on the heartstrings that lured them back to home and hearth, but because they were in 'unfulfilling roles with dim prospects for advancement'. So once again it was not the women but the workplace that presented the main problem.

Many of these well-educated women found that as their careers progressed, they followed the script about how to get ahead. But their efforts met with very different outcomes from their male peers. Although they used career strategies in the same way as men, the lack of results for women climbing the ladder is explained as a female-only affliction. 'Despite the fact that men and women actually have pretty similar career priorities, the belief that women value career less is widespread', the research found. 'At a certain point the belief that a woman's primary career obstacle is herself became conventional wisdom, for both women and men [...] yet framing the conversation this way doesn't reflect reality', the study concluded. I recall a senior female executive telling me that when she missed out on a promotion her boss sat her down to explain that 'the only person who thought she couldn't do the top job was her'. This explanation was not comforting.

Interestingly, the men interviewed for this study had strong expectations that their partners would be the primary caregivers and that their careers would take precedence over their partners'. These expectations, the research rather dryly states, were exceeded. It's a part of the equation we need to keep in mind when the talk about men sharing care and adjusting their time in the workplace comes up. Changing the automatic priority given to male breadwinners means a big shift in expectations – for men and the workplaces that employ them.

Gender bias in selection and promotion practices, rather than women failing to 'lean in', has been the subject of many academic studies over the past decade, but effective interventions in organisations have tended to be few and far between until recently. Even changing the wording in ads has a major impact, as some research in the tech sector has shown. Avoiding heroic and, let's face it, alpha male descriptions is a good step: that means no more 'coding ninjas' or 'gods', which tend to send a signal to women that they are not what a company is looking for.[5]

Sometimes the problem is not the number of women applying for jobs but the number who end up on interview lists. Another Male Champion of Change, Simon Rothery, CEO of investment bank Goldman Sachs Australia, discovered some disturbing homogeneity in his graduate intake a few years ago.

Although young women were applying in reasonable numbers, very few were making the final cut. Partly motivated by his work with the MCC, he decided to investigate what was happening. It turned out the group of employees making the decisions about who to recruit (and who had been graduate recruits themselves not too many years before) were pretty much picking people they felt comfortable with. By intervening and changing the process of selection, the dynamics changed. 'We were selecting private school boys who looked like each other', Rothery told me during a conversation in the Goldman Sachs offices in Sydney in 2016. 'Now the gap has gone and it's 50-50 men and women graduates.'

On the broader question of the selection process for plum jobs, Rothery has been actively appointing women into key and high-profile jobs. Sometimes the moves have been greeted with raised eyebrows. Putting a female banker into a senior role, for example, triggered scepticism, but it has worked out very well, he explained. The appointments, which include a female managing director, have some major benefits internally and externally, in a sector that is not exactly renowned for being female-friendly. 'I think in the market, we are the employer of choice for women who want a career in investment banking and we have senior women in the sector approaching us. I actually think it's a real point of competitive advantage', Rothery said.

One of the best examples of how to circumvent human bias in appointments is the blind audition. The best-known example of this approach emerged some years ago when it was recognised that there were very few female musicians in leading orchestras. It's difficult to fall back on old excuses such as a lack of aptitude, physical prowess or finicky attitudes when it comes to explaining why so few women were deemed good enough at playing a musical instrument. A number of renowned orchestras introduced auditions where applicants played behind a screen to prevent any risk of being identified by gender – with an accompanying significant rise in the number of women appointed.

It's not an easy process to replicate in a business, but an increasing number of examples are emerging in different fields, with the aim of removing other forms of bias too. In fact, UK law firm Clifford Chance decided in 2014 to quietly remove the names of universities on CVs to avoid a bias towards graduates from Oxford and Cambridge in recruiting. The impact was significant: in the first year of the scheme, the annual intake of 100 graduate trainees came from 41 different education institutions – a rise of nearly 30 per cent on the number represented in the previous year under the old recruitment system.[6]

An interesting array of examples have emerged in Australia from applying the same principle. The Australian Bureau of Statistics used the approach to help double the number of women in its ranks, along with asking women what they wanted from their jobs.[7] By removing names and other identifying details of applicants, there was a relatively fast boost: the number of women in senior jobs was hovering at 21 per cent before the 2015 hiring drive, which resulted in women making up 350 of the 613 successful applicants, who now make up 43 per cent of senior executives. Other Australian companies are following suit, with retail bank Westpac announcing a new trial of the approach in 2016, along with the Victorian public service. As my former colleague Fiona Smith noted, the government-initiated project to use blind or anonymous hiring is being trialled by a total of 29 large public and private sector organisations including

Deloitte, Ernst & Young, Australia Post, Dow Chemical, PwC and Victoria Police.[8] In the UK, the civil service uses the same approach to help bypass bias in recruitment and in Canada the concept has also been considered.[9]

While it is a circuit breaker, blind recruitment is no silver bullet. Psychologist and consultant Jennifer Whelan says the process has caught on like wildfire, but sounds a note of caution. 'Of course it is only effective for senior roles if women have had access to the same development opportunities as their male peers, because if they haven't then they won't look as capable at senior levels.' Just because you get more women on a long or even short list doesn't guarantee success, so while it's a good first step, other measures to address bias are also needed to decide who gets the job.

Finally, no discussion about this area can ignore the crucial impact the concept of merit plays in determining who gets considered, much less appointed to a role (more on this in chapter 5). It's a term that has effectively disguised high degrees of subjectivity behind an illusion of objectivity for decades. I was told by a female director that a male colleague of hers many years ago often said 'merit' was really an acronym for Mates Elevated Regardless of Intellect or Talent. That's a definition I suspect is not uppermost in the minds of those who firmly argue merit is the only criteria used to appoint anyone to a job. Ever. That stance is becoming hard to sustain as the ranks of well-educated and qualified women in organisations swell, while the number making it up the ladder stagnates. But mentioning merit is still a highly effective way to derail discussions on addressing bias.

And it doesn't help to challenge the merit myth when there's a rather passive approach to job selection in many workplaces, as

Martin Parkinson, head of the Australian Department of Prime Minister and Cabinet, pointed out. 'I suspect one culprit is that, when hiring staff, we interpret merit as belonging to the person we could immediately put into a job as a safe pair of hands. We don't tend to think of merit as the potential a candidate has, or their capacity to learn. We also probably don't focus on building a deeper pool of candidates. A recruitment panel's success should be judged on getting about 50-50 gender balance in applications. It's not a panel's job to sit back and wait for the applications to roll in, it's their job to go out and find good candidates.'[10]

A number of top businesses have started taking steps to redefine merit. Qantas, the Australian Army, KPMG and ANZ are all included as case studies in a report, 'In the eye of the beholder: avoiding the merit trap', released in late 2016 by the Male Champions of Change and Chief Executive Women. At Qantas, excuses for not meeting gender targets hinged on a lack of women with specific technical skills outlined in job descriptions, so the requirements were rewritten and more focus put on areas such as leadership qualities. More women were able to enter the pipeline for management, and there was a 2 per cent improvement in senior women appointed in 2015/16. One of the significant examples was the appointment of Jetstar's first female pilot, Georgina Sutton, who was recognised and promoted for her technical skills and leadership credentials from her role as fleet captain of the 737 fleet. Sometimes the net needs to be thrown a little more widely to find the best candidates.

At an unusually frank discussion on merit to launch the report, Commonwealth Bank CEO Ian Narev was forthright about the backlash that often occurs, consisting of complaints about merit being compromised, when there are programs to support women. Those who get most hot and bothered by this are often men in middle management, 'But at a certain point, if you're a senior male and you genuinely believe that an appointment's been made other than on merit, and you genuinely believe you won't get a chance because you're a male, you're probably not a good fit any more. If people are starting to whinge about "It's getting tough here", then boy, that's not the top ten list of tough things going on. And it's kind of like, if you can't adjust, there's a bit of a selection process.'[11] Fellow bank CEO, ANZ's Shane Elliott, said fear about job losses drives a lot of the seething. 'There is an absolute backlash of middle management males who […] resent the fact that in their mind we are choosing diversity candidates over merit. Now, they may not use that word "merit", but it is absolutely apparent. And it's quite a strongly held view.'

Key decision-making processes for promotions have also been examined in the army (more on this in chapter 7). The composition of the Personnel Advisory Committees, that review and recommend officers and soldiers for advancement, was changed to include more women and external observers, which is unusual. The observers encouraged the panels to question assumptions about the reputation of candidates and the idea there was a 'golden road' to promotion. The result was a 2 per cent increase in women promoted to senior roles in the four years to 2016.

What some of these leaders are grasping is that publicly describing organisations as meritocracies doesn't automatically make them so – in fact it may actually do more harm than good. One of the best-known studies on merit, conducted by Emilio Castilla and Stephen Benard, found 'when an organizational culture promotes meritocracy (compared with when it does not), managers in that organization may ironically show greater bias in favor of men over equally performing women in translating employee performance evaluations into rewards and other key career outcomes; we call this the "paradox of meritocracy"'.[12]

The assumption that women routinely sabotage their chances of getting a job or promotion by failing to have or display the elusive components of merit is being robustly challenged by the interventions outlined in this chapter. No single solution is the answer, but the growing appetite for new ways of running basic recruitment processes is significant. The penny is dropping that key steps which many employees have long assumed were neutral and entirely based on a cold, hard assessment of tangible factors are actually riddled with subjectivity and, in many cases, bias. Investigating the criteria for appointments, particularly at senior levels, can reveal they have often been modelled on past incumbents and in many cases there's a good statistical chance that will have been a man, and so another man can appear to be the best match.

As the results and examples in this chapter show, there can be a reasonably fast transformation when gender as an initial sorting mechanism is removed and there are efforts to redefine and recognise a broader range of job requirements, skills and experience. These are essential steps to address remedial attitudes and discrimination in deciding who gets the job, and crucial for action on the closely related problem of who gets the money, which we turn to now.

CHAPTER 4

Earning power

'We'll never solve the feminization
of power until we solve the
masculinity of wealth.'

GLORIA STEINEM

I GOT TEN CENTS A week as pocket money when I was a child. While that amount tells you quite a bit about my age, and my parents' strict budgeting, the point is that I recall my brothers got the same amount. Which means I was doing pretty well. Turns out girls often don't do as well as boys in the same family when the weekly allowance is handed out, according to research from a number of countries. And the really bad news is that the gender gap, even at this tender age, may be widening. Boys in the UK were 12 per cent better off in their pocket money than girls in 2016, according to a study by Halifax bank, compared to a 2 per cent difference in 2015.[1] A similar blitz of data over recent years shows that in some countries graduates face a gender pay gap just a year after joining the workforce, with some surveys showing a difference of up to 10 per cent between young women and men.

Yet many vocal critics continue to insist that the gender pay gap isn't real. Or that it relies on faulty assumptions and can be mainly blamed on motherhood. But gaps in pocket money and graduate pay get a more muted response from the naysayers because it's hard to believe those rationales apply. Confusion continues to characterise discussions about pay and gender and it's quite possible the gap – and its multi-layered effects – could qualify as the most poorly understood of a bunch of red-flag gender topics. It makes even data crunchers tense and angry and sometimes quite irrational – it simply doesn't add up to blame systemic pay differences in all sorts of jobs and sectors on women's poor negotiating skills. And I certainly don't recall sitting down with my parents to nut out an appropriate level of pocket money. This reaction reflects the importance of an arena where we have the clearest and most compelling evidence of how sexism and discrimination have an impact on something tangible – the hip pocket. What we get paid also, of course, reflects the value of what we do – and that's where it all gets very tricky for women.

There are several areas of particular concern about women and money – whether it is pay, income and access to capital for a business, or retirement savings. Each area is worth examining to analyse whether this increasingly well-documented penalty for women can still be blamed on them; and what is being done by employers to intervene and change the dynamics of who gets the money.

Having had more conversations about gender and pay than most, Yolanda Beattie is a worthy voice to heed on this topic. The former Strategy and Engagement Executive Manager at the Workplace Gender Equality Agency (WGEA), she now runs a diversity practice for consulting firm Mercer. She's fed up with being told the pay gap is a myth and instead describes it as probably the most miscommunicated and misinterpreted concept in gender economics.

In three years at the WGEA, Beattie gave countless media interviews explaining the gender pay gap and always started with what it's not: an apples-for-apples comparison. Instead, it's the average salary of women expressed as a percentage of the average salary of men.

'But that doesn't mean that the gap isn't "gendered". Australian women earn on average around 18 per cent less than Australian men for reasons that are largely attributed to their gender – time taken to care, stereotypes ingrained from birth about roles women and men should do, and lack of flexible work in senior roles to help women manage their disproportionate caring responsibilities are among these gendered reasons. And they're gendered by definition because they overwhelmingly impact women and their earnings more than men. They lead to a near 40 per cent gap in retirement savings and explain why women are more than two times more likely than men to retire into poverty. It's these sobering statistics that surely debunk any claim of rationality.'[2]

In early 2016 a piece of research hit the headlines and revealed a sadly depressing picture around gender and pay which was nevertheless a welcome addition to this debate. In a very small nutshell, it was found that when women enter fields in greater numbers than men, the pay levels decrease. In one deft data moment the idea that women deserve (and effectively opt for) lower pay because they 'choose' less lucrative jobs that suit them better was turned on its head. The pay in nursing and teaching isn't low in comparison to other sectors by accident or because women are better at 'caring' roles; the wages are lousy because these jobs are dominated by women, whose work is undervalued. This was not a small study, either, with the research using US census data from 1950 to 2000.[3] The results confirm a troubling reality, according to New York Times journalist Claire Cain Miller, which is that 'work done by women simply isn't valued as highly'.[4]

Rather than women bringing less skill and experience to jobs in some sectors, the shift to a more female-dominated workforce sees employers putting a lower value on the work done by women, Miller points out. Sectors examined in the research included the field of recreation – jobs in parks and camps – where a shift in the predominant gender of the workforce from men to women saw hourly wages drop by 57 per cent in the US. In computer programming, the opposite has happened: as men came to outnumber women, the roles became more prestigious and the pay increased. Although the same dynamic is not occurring in white-collar jobs, the pay gap is still very large there, which the researchers believe may be a function of long hours and lack of flexibility for workers, who may be penalised for taking flexible work options.

The results certainly rang a bell with me, as I've heard about the same phenomena of wage decreases or increases being linked to less or more feminisation over many years. A senior woman in the industry superannuation fund sector once told me she was astonished to see the pay increases in her area as it grew, its status increased and more men entered the field. Now there is robust data to back this observation up and provide much-needed evidence about the way pay gaps emerge. It flies in the face of a host of excuses: that the data is faulty or exaggerated, that part-time hours are compared to full-time, that women don't ask for pay rises and opt for jobs in sectors that just don't pay well. Or that maternity leave and parenting roles are the only reasons for the discrepancy. There's a familiar theme here: the fault lies again with women.

While motherhood certainly has an effect on pay (often dubbed the maternal penalty), parenthood doesn't seem to have the same impact on dads. Fathers working full-time get paid a fifth more than men with similar jobs who don't have children, according to a 2016 report by the UK Trade Union Council. This average, a 21 per cent 'wage bonus', is 'in stark contrast to the experience of working mothers', says the report. Women who become mothers before age 33 typically suffer a 15 per cent pay penalty.[5] The diehards will no doubt explain this is because fathers can work longer hours and mothers tend to take flexible work. But the wage bonus is substantial, even allowing for some discrepancy in time spent in paid work. Actually, pay gap data takes into account the hours worked by men and women, so the findings are not distorted in the broadest average figures. And although we do know that Australian women in general spend fewer hours than men in paid work – with many in part-time roles – they do spend a third more time than men working in the home and in caring roles. Added together, full-time working women spend 6.4 hours more per week working inside and out-side the home than full-time working men. Averaged across the year, this means a 332 additional hours (or two weeks of 24-hour days) of work.[6]

And unpaid work is in fact worth a lot to society. In 2006, the total value of unpaid household work in Australia was $392 billion. Women did about 64 per cent of it, spending on average 12 per cent of their day on domestic activities.[7] It's much the same division of labour in the US, where data 'show a large and lasting gender gap. Women do more housework than men even when they are more educated, work full-time and are more egalitarian. In fact, some studies show women spend more time in housework even when their husbands earn less money or stay at home'.[8] And the sting in the tail is that extra domestic work is rarely deemed as serious or 'real' work. This is even though it is clearly essential, not just for the family and household, but to prop up a traditional male breadwinner in today's demanding workplaces. Many women could really do with having a 'wife', as Annabel Crabb pointed out in her book *The Wife Drought*.

With the extra domestic load to handle, shrinking the time spent in paid work (if you can afford it) becomes a necessity, not a choice for women. But even when women work similar hours to men they take home less pay at management level. Once you get to senior ranks, everyone is under pressure to perform and work similarly long hours. Few executives survive without some confidence (more on this in chapter 8) and a sense of what they are worth, which surely suggests some other reasons are at play. In fact, women working full-time in key management personnel jobs were earning $100 000 less per year than their male peers, according to 2016 Australian data. The gaps were 'significant across all management categories and grow in accordance with seniority', the research from the WGEA revealed.[9]

The gap persists, regardless of tenure and experience. Even if women move through management levels at the same rate as men, working full-time and reaching their key management job in their tenth year, they are still well behind men in earning capacity: men would have earned $2.3 million and women $1.7 million in base salary. The same data, by the way, also reveal that far from being a marginal issue, getting more women onto boards has an impact on reducing the gender pay gap. With equal numbers of male and female directors on a board, there is a 6.3 per cent drop in the pay gap for full-time managers.

And then there's the notion that any gap just comes down to women failing to ask for more. While this piece of deficit folklore does have some backing from research, many studies have also shown that negotiating a pay rise is not a simple process for women (and of course many women in low-skill jobs don't get the chance to negotiate). It's often a no-win situation (as we'll soon see from several studies) because if women ask for nothing then they usually get nothing, but ask too assertively and they can be marked down for being aggressive. Which brings up another part of the already tricky pay gap negotiation: the opaque area of discretionary pay, which may be a bonus or incentive payment, and can be a substantial part of a pay packet for management jobs but also for those working in sales roles.

Bonus pay is usually cloaked in secrecy, which makes it even harder to know whether gender factors are having an impact. But the WGEA has now been able to reveal that men in Australian businesses 'consistently earn more additional remuneration than women. Women working full-time are paid an average additional 18.1 per cent of their base salary in extras and men an additional 25 per cent of their base salary. That leads to an average male "bonus" premium of almost 8 percentage points for full-time workers.' And the sector where this premium is highest for men? Financial and insurance services, which comes in with a hefty extra 15 percentage points for male employees. This is depressing stuff (and you'd really think employees in financial services would be good at crunching numbers). It seems to indicate that a wide gap opens up when there is the potential for subjective assessments of who is deserving. That's not ideal if you happen to be a woman, even if you are as feisty as the experts tell you is mandatory.

But there are ways to break the circuit around bonus pay, even in investment banking. A few years ago, Simon Rothery, CEO of Goldman Sachs Australia, saw the annual queue of employees forming outside his office, which could only mean one thing – it was bonus time again. The season when a substantial number of his employees felt an overwhelming urge to sit down and tell him how wonderful and, well, deserving they really were. Not one woman ever appeared in that conga line, he said. And although there were many reasons for his decision to cut out individual lobbying altogether, it was also clear to him the process did the women in the firm no favours. 'I just don't do it [now] and it worked against the people who did it anyway because I didn't want to do it. Men are just better self-promoters', Rothery tells me. Well, they are certainly encouraged to be – just as many women feel they are frowned on for behaving in the same way.

And what of the effect on gender pay equity? Although Rothery can't divulge too much detail, the gap, he says, has gone. 'We do look at it and there is no gap [...] one of the reasons there is a gap at any firm is the men will call up and say, "I have an offer from Macquarie (Bank) and I want another $10 000" but we don't budge and it's the same for men and women. We're performance driven and it's easy to check on pay.' As we'll soon see, a number of companies are also taking formal steps to eradicate the gender pay gap by changing the systems, not the women.

Removing the 'beauty parade' dynamic for bonus negotiations at Goldman Sachs Australia involved recognising that the way men were behaving wasn't effective and it excluded women. It has also circumvented the possibility of some pretty vicious double standards around women and assertive behaviour – as any mother, female prime minister or female manager will tell you. When he's bossy or pushy it's just part of the deal; when she is, it's the height of bitchiness and a betrayal of the sisterhood. And that dynamic is the case for women in all kinds of jobs, and not just the management level.

This gendered disadvantage isn't just conjecture. There are binders of research that show how a simple-sounding piece of behavioural advice for women to 'act more confident' in pay negotiations can go horribly wrong when there's no even playing field. An experiment by Laurie Rudman of Rutgers and Peter Glick of Lawrence University and written up by consulting firm McKinsey asked participants how they would respond if a job candidate gave a very confident reply to how they would respond under pressure.[10] The results found the assessment of the candidate differed enormously depending on their gender. 'They found that when a man who was presented as assertive delivered this response, he was seen as confident and competent;

observers said they would want to hire him. But when a woman described as assertive made the same self-promotional statements, she was viewed as less likable and not a good fit for the job.' That sounds like a minefield for women, no matter what they do. If this is the reaction, then it's no wonder men are seen as 'better' self-promoters, as Simon Rothery points out.

There is a very real risk and punishment for women if they are not seen as 'nice', the same research points out. 'Because women as a group have less power than men, they face an additional barrier to using power – women are expected to be communal, caring, and submissive. These societal expectations produce an unfortunate double bind: when women do feel and project power, they are punished. Women need to act with confidence to get ahead. But when they do, they face a potential backlash.'

More research by Carnegie Mellon's Linda Babcock and Harvard's Hannah Riley Bowles found 'women are right to be cautious about asking. Across multiple studies, they explored what happens when men and women behave assertively in salary negotiations. Even when the sexes engage in exactly the same behavior, women get punished for not accepting first offers and for requesting more'.[11]

It also turns out that although it may have been true in the past, these days women do in fact ask for pay rises as often as men, according to a 2016 study of Australian data by researchers at London's Cass Business School, the University of Warwick, and the University of Wisconsin. Women were, however, 25 per cent less likely than men to get the raise. The research also revealed women were not generally concerned about upsetting their boss by asking. 'These findings shift the burden from professional women to the companies that employ them. These days, it appears that closing the pay gap may be less about changing the ways women have been raised to understand the value of their work and more about how their employers react to women's improving negotiating skills.'[12]

There is of course another brake on women's earnings and it's their propensity to take time out for family responsibilities – not that they usually have many viable alternatives. The impact on their pay following maternity leave, as mentioned, is significant and disproportionate because it doesn't just reflect a period out of the workplace when you might miss out on further experience. In fact I've noticed that when colleagues have left their jobs for travel or a break they were not seen as completely out-of-touch when they returned, or drained of all previous expertise. But mothers face a lot of assumptions about their dedication and ability to cope. Worse, the maternal pay penalty actually compounds over the years, rather than recovering at some point. And in fact, broken tenure in paid work is the obvious main culprit for women ending up with far less money than men after they retire (more on this soon).

Women starting their own business when they have children – dubbed the 'mumpreneurs' – don't necessarily avoid problems with income either. In fact it can add to longer term financial insecurity. About two-thirds of the women surveyed by Dr Meraiah Foley for her study of maternal self-employment (mentioned in chapter 1) cited inflexible work schedules, poor-quality part-time jobs, and discriminatory attitudes towards part-time and flexible workers as the main push factors for their shift. Among these were six women who were made redundant while pregnant or on maternity leave, echoing findings from the Australian Human Rights Commission that women with children still face high levels of discrimination in Australian workplaces. Nearly two-thirds of these women were not contributing to superannuation. And they struggled to re-enter the job market if their business failed, because the time running the business was seen as time out of work by employers.[13]

Given all of this data, checking on pay levels to ensure a gap doesn't exist or emerge seems like a good idea. While it can be time consuming, the use of pay audits to detect gender gaps is becoming quite well established. I've never heard of an audit that didn't detect a gender pay gap, despite also hearing every rationalisation under the sun. And pay audits don't begin by blaming women for the disparity in the money they earn, or rely on the deficit model as an explanation that often leads to another series of remedial responses. Once a gap is identified, the solutions are also reasonably straightforward – more pay to those who are missing out is a pretty obvious first step, of course, but recalibrating the way performance is assessed and rewarded is the next cab off the rank. And although more organisations need to get with the pay audit program, the numbers of companies taking part are increasing. In 2015 a report from WGEA found that there was a welcome rise in the number of employers running pay gap analyses.[14] A total of 1229 organisations reported that in 2015 they had conducted a gender pay gap analysis, compared with 1045 in 2014 – a 17.6 per cent increase; 26.3 per cent of all reporting organisations said they had conducted a pay gap analysis, up from 24 per cent; and 51 per cent of organisations that conducted a gender pay gap analysis took action to address pay imbalances, up from 46 per cent.

One of the companies taking action on the pay gap is logistics group Asciano (now Qube), which has used the WGEA reporting process on gender to monitor gender pay equity and close gender pay gaps. After identifying a double-digit gender pay gap among managers in 2013, Asciano implemented a number of proactive strategies, including embedding gender targets in manager KPIs, leadership programs for women, and actively closing pay gaps during remuneration reviews, WGEA reported in 2016.[15]

The 2015 findings on pay gap analysis came a year after the Agency launched its pioneering campaign – In Your Hands – which aimed to encourage and help CEOs address their like-for-like gender pay gaps by undertaking a gender pay gap analysis and addressing gender bias in performance assessment, talent management and pay decisions.[16] Action most often included: identifying causes of the gaps; reviewing remuneration decision-making processes; and reporting pay equity metrics to the executive. Around a quarter of employers said they didn't find any inexplicable or unjustifiable gaps. But less than 10 per cent report to the board on pay equity, 7.4 per cent train people managers in addressing gender bias, and 15.6 per cent analyse performance pay to ensure there's no gender bias. The report also found organisations that included pay equity objectives in their pay policies had increased from 18.1 per cent to 25.6 per cent in 2015. The findings were based on data provided to WGEA by over 11 000 employers who represented around 4 million employees – over a third of the Australian workforce.

Intervening to change the dynamics around pay is tricky, but there are some fundamentals that have been effective. Aside from examples such as cutting out the bonus negotiations at Goldman Sachs Australia, a number of formal steps can change the processes around how remuneration is set. Pay levels can be deliberately opaque in many organisations, so injecting more transparency is actually a very good place to start. In the public sector, where pay scales are published, the gender pay gap is often substantially lower than in the private sector: in Australia the gap is more like 12 per cent than the 18 per cent recorded in in the business sector.

The momentum for addressing pay gaps is building. Commonwealth Bank's 2015 pay equity review triggered the introduction of a range of new measures, including ensuring employees on parental leave don't miss out on pay and performance reviews, as well as targeting 'hot spots' in an employee's career or 'life cycle'.[17] CEO Ian Narev said the bank monitored and analysed talent management data, including pay, by gender and was taking action where necessary. One of the factors revealed was that comparing aggregate like-for-like jobs did not show a gap, but more detailed analysis found a series of areas for possible bias – including new hires, employees on extended leave and performance ratings (which is where highly subjective ideas about merit and leadership skills can contribute to bias; see chapter 3).

Some years ago I was impressed to see a young woman, Katie-Jeyn Romeyn, accept an award from the WGEA for her work bridging the gender pay gap at listed gold mining company, St Barbara. The results were outstanding. Having interviewed Romeyn for my last book, I was interested in finding out in 2016 whether she thought other sectors had begun to realise they needed to address the pay gap and how to go about it.

After leaving St Barbara in 2014, Romeyn had set up her own business, Coach on Collins, and was finding the embedded attitudes about the gender pay gap, and whether it even exists, were still firmly rusted on in many places. 'The challenge is many leaders don't realise they actually have a problem', she told me when we caught up. 'I met with the CEO of a particular company recently and he handed me to his HR manager, who had the mindset that everything they are doing is the right thing. The HR manager said: "We don't have a problem with pay equity because we treat everybody the same and on merit". But they did have a problem because they remunerate on longevity. And this is common.'

What has consistently emerged from analysis and vetting of remuneration data was that the ability to set pay between certain amounts – in a salary band – for some roles was a major culprit. Because there was discretion to allocate the level of pay between those parameters, new employees often start at the lower level of the band than others, which means it can be difficult to catch up. 'When setting remuneration the number one priority is that employees must be paid at the minimum of the band and then after their reviews get a percentage increase based on performance. Then you have to see if people are where they should be in the band relative to peers. Then you go back to the data and look at gender.'

There's still a fundamental idea that pay equity is only a comparison of very similar roles (like-for-like) but that is an over-simplification, she explained. 'I had that thinking when I first started at St Barbara but leaders must progress beyond that and look at the overall gap and the systemic issues and how people perform – including those that have been there a long time. Generally they are not the high performers.' Not that cracking the pay gap is easy for anyone. Some of the 'aha' moments and best results came from challenging and cranky discussions, she said. And some organisations are doing the right things: starting by addressing like-for-like pay, moving to salary bands then on to bigger systemic and cultural changes.

Interestingly, the gender pay gap isn't worst in mining companies like St Barbara. Financial services, as I noted earlier, tends to get top honours. So it was fascinating when I heard Gary Wingrove, the CEO of professional services firm KPMG Australia, talk about the firm's initial reaction to the idea that a gap could be right under their nose – a fair bit of denial. In 2011 the firm started to look at the breakdown of salaries and discovered, to the senior team's surprise, that there was a gap. 'The first time that the issue of pay equity came to our executive team in 2012, many of us said we couldn't have a gender [pay] differential. What we found out when we analysed it in detail, which we now do every time we go through pay review and promotion cycles, is that we did have a difference. So we set about addressing that.'[18] By 2015 the audit was on name-by-name basis, according to HR managing partner Susan Ferrier, who called the pay equity gap 'the scourge of the 21st century'.[19]

By 2016, KPMG, which employs about 6500 people in Australia, had got its gender pay gap down from 6 per cent to just over 1 per cent, Wingrove told me at a forum to mark International Women's Day. Another financial services firm, PwC, reported to WGEA that running a gender pay gap audit revealed an organisation-wide gender pay gap of 11.4 per cent in favour of men. PwC attributed the gender pay gap to a range of factors such as the low representation of women in senior positions, including the 18 per cent share of partnerships held by women. As a result of the audit, PwC has adopted a target for a minimum of 40 per cent women and 40 per cent men making up future partner intakes, and resolved to be stringent in its annual remuneration reviews.

When the problems around the pay gap, or the tangle of red tape and lack of flexibility in an organisation, become just too hard, more and more women are starting up their own enterprises in the hope of finding more control and less bias in earning an income (as I examined in chapter 1). I've interviewed a lot of women in the small to medium enterprise area over the years and many have similar stories of being frustrated by the rigid workplace regime and lack of progression at larger employers, and the need to set their own rules. Although more women are taking this option in the hope of circumventing the bias, getting access to capital for their enterprise, no matter its size, can be a stumbling block. And those in the startup space find the going even tougher.

Some of the issues that make pay equity a problem in large organisations can cause other kinds of financial disadvantages for women in small business too. Gender bias is a barrier for women in small business, according to more than half (51.3 per cent) of female respondents in a 2015 survey by Westpac.[20] And 57.3 per cent of female small business owners identified 'financial constraints' as an additional barrier faced by women in the sector. The story is similar in the US. Lack of access to capital or government contracts are barriers faced by US women in the small business arena that differ from those that confront women employees, but the underlying causes are similar, according to a study. It suggests 'that women in the United States carry their labor market disadvantage with them to the small business sphere, where it is compounded by new manifestations of the same institutional barriers.'[21]

Women tend to start up a business with low levels of capital. A survey of Australian female business operators found that 66 per cent of women's startup funds were sourced from personal savings and 25 per cent from a credit card or bank/ credit union loan.[22] The survey also found that 42 per cent of respondents started their business with less than $5000, while 83 per cent did so with less than $100 000. More data from 2010 research on women's access to business finance in Australia found that men and women did not differ significantly in their demand for business finance or the types of finance they used. It did, however, point out that young and home-based firms were the ones that typically faced difficulties accessing finance, and these firms were more likely to be owned by women. The study also showed that women were slightly less likely than men to report that their firm was profitable in recent years, and slightly more likely to report moderate or high debt levels.[23] Difficulties getting access to finance is even more pronounced for women looking at venture capital or funds for a startup. The problems have motivated concerned observers to form a few organisations to help women establish either the connections to get the right backing, such as Heads Over Heels (mentioned in chapter 1), or to access capital such as Springboard, which quotes that only 1.7 per cent of the billions in venture capital investments made in 1997 had been invested in women-led businesses. The non-profit was set up in 1999, and is 'dedicated to accelerating women entrepreneurs' access to the equity markets'.[24]

Some of the reasons women find raising funds for a new venture or small business an uphill battle include: difficulty in accessing capital, and receiving a smaller proportion of venture capital; they start with less capital; and they may be fighting bias and have less of a track record, which does not impress investors.[25] And there is a particularly worrying outlook for women in small business when it comes to retirement savings. When women earn less, they save less; and when they have broken working lives from taking longer breaks to care for others, they usually end up with far less in their old age than they need. This depressing scenario has appalling outcomes for many women, not just in the past but right now. And it's particularly punitive for those who have little choice but to do what they were told was the right thing – to make caring a priority in their lives. As Elizabeth Broderick, gender adviser and former Sex Discrimination Commissioner, is often asked: is poverty the reward for a lifetime of care?

There's a dismal picture for most women heading to retirement in Australia. They have on average retirement savings of about 45 per cent of men's – or less than half, according to the aptly titled report 'A husband is not a retirement plan' on a Senate inquiry into women's economic security in retirement.[26] And the figure is worse if you are self-employed – about 75 per cent of self-employed women have either no superannuation savings, or savings of less than $40 000, according to the Association of Superannuation Funds of Australia. The average superannuation balance of self-employed women aged 60–64 was estimated at $69 000 in 2011–12, about half the balance for female wage and salary earners in the same age group. Nearly half of all owner-operated small businesses in Australia do not survive their first three years, the Bureau of Statistics says. And there is ample evidence that self-employed mothers face particular barriers when it comes to re-entering the job market – as both working mothers and 'failed' entrepreneurs.[27] Building up retirement funds can seem a low priority when you are trying to make up for time out of the workplace or covering the cost of childcare. It's often a perfect storm of circumstances that leaves women well behind their male peers from relatively early in their working lives.

No wonder that the difference in balances at retirement was $197 000 for men on average and $105 000 for women in 2011–12. Women also accumulate less wealth and assets over their life-times, which is caused not just by the gender pay gap and related factors but the negative effects of single parenthood and barriers to accumulating wealth for those from migrant backgrounds or in rural areas, the report pointed out. Older single women are one of the fastest growing cohorts of people living in poverty in Australia: 38.7 per cent of this group.[28]

Refreshingly, however, the report looked at a broad range of social, economic and workplace issues that intersected to make it difficult for women to save for retirement, rather than blaming women for making poor decisions, 'choosing' lower paid jobs and taking time off for caring. It examined the struc-tural causes and the changes needed to make the system fairer. But it also highlighted a key point: the problems that contrib-ute to this serious financial shortfall for women is not just a legacy issue or a problem that will gradually resolve itself. 'The forces that lead to the differences between women's and men's patterns of work continue to act on young women today', the report pointed out.

Australia's retirement income system structurally favours higher income earners who work full-time, without breaks, for the entirety of their working life. The women (and men) who do not fit this pattern of work face a significant handicap when saving for their retirement.

'Australia needs to redouble its efforts to achieve equality at work – paying women equally, offering access to career development and leadership opportunities, and accommodating rather than penalising those who care for others. Government, business, and individuals have a role to play in achieving women's full participation in our workplaces.'

The gender pay gap clearly plays a key and continuing role in the poor level of savings women accrue, as the report noted. In particular, the problems with compounding penalties on women's lifetime earnings for taking time out to care for families is well documented. One of the ways to address the shortfall in savings by women in the short term is to top up their accounts. Rice Warner, a small consulting firm, and retail bank ANZ have both taken this approach. The ANZ scheme is a 1 per cent annual payment to women whose retirement savings are below $50 000. Rice Warner pays its female employees an extra 2 per cent on top of their superannuation guarantee payments.

Both employers acknowledged to the inquiry that the step was not perfect nor a long-term structural solution to the savings problem, but it's a measure that is tangible and has practical results. Michael Rice, CEO of Rice Warner, told the inquiry that he knew there would be an outcry that the move was unfair. He pointed out that the company pays insurance for all staff and while male insurance was more expensive, 'no-one ever complains about that'. Having spoken to Michael a few times about this, I can vouch for his dedication to this approach and energetic dismissal of the naysayers.

At ANZ the impetus for the superannuation top-up came from a number of places, including the then head of global wealth Joyce Phillips (who left ANZ in early 2016). A strong advocate for change, she helped devise and launch a major campaign called Equal Future to promote better understanding of the barriers facing women in securing their financial future (full disclosure: I was involved in the program and wrote a regular column called 'Enough' for the ANZ Women website on ways to combat sexism and bias in daily working life). It was appreciating how the structures and systems hampered women from the time they are girls that got Phillips annoyed and prompted her to come up with the campaign, complete with a television commercial directed by renowned New Zealand film maker Jane Campion. It wasn't an easy sell to the top executives but she persevered and the campaign went viral on social media, catapulting ANZ to the top of the financial services brands.

Over a glass of wine one evening in Sydney she told me how fed up she was with being told that the reasons many women were in poor financial health was because there was something wrong with them. 'We get told we will never get ahead unless we act like a man – well, I've never done that. Women can lead like women and it's very effective.' But beyond individual behaviour, as she pointed out, much more intervention is needed to get women on an even footing or the retirement savings landscape will continue to leave many in a bleak position. And Phillips is an advocate of greater transparency on some other key indicators on gender: she would like to see listed companies publish the number of women on the board, the number of direct reports to the CEO, and the total compensation divided by the number of women at senior levels.[28]

There are rays of light, then, in the middle of the sombre news on retirement savings for women. The level of understanding about superannuation gender inequity has improved dramatically since I started writing about the topic. In fact, some of my first columns for the *Financial Review* were about fledgling attempts to address the low level of savings women had in comparison to men. Along with this deeper appreciation of the hurdles women face is an increasing appreciation that telling women to just get more financially literate in the face of structural inequity can be both patronising and ultimately ineffectual. And anyway, as some of the participants in the inquiry noted, even if women have more knowledge about superannuation, many lower income earners would still not have enough money to contribute. Women in Super's Sandra Buckley 'dismissed arguments that women do not have sufficient financial literacy' and said studies they had run to survey levels of understanding of this topic found women did know about super and were worried about how much they had in savings. Many were running family finances and were 'acutely aware of the problems they face in trying to accumulate more superannuation', according to the report.

So here's the thing about tackling the gender pay gap: it can be done. A pay audit is not a magic spell or even the final answer but it is a concrete first step to reveal what is happening and to then formulate steps to address the problem. Smart companies are now providing women on maternity leave with the ability to continue their retirement contributions; other employers, as we have seen, have gone even further by topping up women's superannuation balances, having worked out that a relatively modest outlay has a big impact on individuals and reputation.

The eminent US economist Claudia Goldin has spent decades researching and setting the debate around gender and economics. In a podcast for Freakonomics, she outlined some of the main reasons for the gender pay gap and some misconceptions about the role of bias and discrimination. Asked for the best approach to dealing with it, such as changing attitudes and behaviour by men in the workplace, she replied, 'I think that it would be easier to accomplish getting the price of the amenity down, than [...] reprogramming all the men in the United States. So, I think of these issues as these solutions in buckets as: fix the women – that is, make them more competitive, better bargaining skills, better at math. Fix the infants – take care of the infants, that will do it, OK? Fix the men – which is the point that we were just talking about. Or, fix the organizations and the jobs, and I'm thinking more about the latter.'[29]

To put it another way, it's the structures: the performance assessments used to determine who is doing a good job, the judgement of who should do what work, how much value that work has, the ability to conform to linear tenure models and the way we are expected to save for retirement. The evidence shows that when it comes to earning income, whether as an employee or in a small business, asking for money is a fraught affair for women. Once they are mothers, women face another wall of penalties, while for fathers, as we've seen, there is a parenting bonus. This complicated scenario reflects not just workplace attitudes but strong social norms about who should bring home the bacon. And it is not likely to be fixed or even changed at all by sending women to learn how to be alpha males; it would be much more useful, in fact, to spend the time analysing the effectiveness of the aggressive masculine behaviour that is considered desirable in pay negotiations.

There are no easy paths to bridging the gender pay gap, but

examples are building that show some interventions can be highly effective. And they can be measured. Data on pay and other gender indicators, along with targets for making a difference in the numbers of women in certain jobs, have been a circuit breaker in the business world, as the next chapter examines. And the debate about the efficacy or otherwise of mandatory measures, such as quotas, offers a fresh insight into the tenacity of the deficit model at work. Proof is not the only weapon for changing minds, but it is needed to show why unpopular interventions have to be made, as we will see.

CHAPTER 5

How targets build meritocracies

'One woman is a token;
two women a conspiracy and
three make a difference.'

POPULAR ADAGE

THERE WAS A RIPPLE OF surprise and apprehension in the business community in mid-2016 when the chair of the Australian Institute of Company Directors (AICD), Elizabeth Proust, said that quotas would have to be on the table if a target of 30 per cent women on listed company boards was not a reality by 2018.[1] The pros and cons of imposing a gender goal for powerful enclaves, whether listed company boards or legislative bodies, are hotly debated in many parts of the world. The naysayers believe the downsides of forced measures far outweigh the advantages, supporters see them as a necessary circuit-breaker to speed up the slow progress in appointing women when companies rely on voluntary compliance regimes. But the fact that there is a discussion at all, and that progress can be more accurately mapped, reflects a transformation. Not too long ago the question wasn't about quotas but whether gender inequity even existed or was simply a result of women not wanting or trying hard enough to make the grade.

Thankfully, a comprehensive amount of regular data on gender is now routinely being captured and provided. The AICD even updates the statistics about women on boards in real time – one of the only organisations in the world to do so; no doubt to ensure the progress from voluntary compliance is transparent and acts as an incentive. It's all a world away from when I started writing about women and the workforce in the early 1990s, when there was precious little information on the gender markers we now take for granted. Whether it was the percentage of women in management (it was never hard to check the number of CEOs: there were so few they could fit in a Tarago), or the gender pay gap or the difference in the level of superannuation savings between men and women, the data just wasn't around.

That's all changed for the better. Measurement and reporting on these areas reflects a new level of attention to how women are faring in the workplace – although some of the reporting in Australia is an obligation. From the reporting guidelines issued by the Australian Securities Exchange's Corporate Governance Council, which stipulate annual publication of gender numbers and women in management, to the regular breakdown of reporting from 11 000 organisations by the Workplace Gender Equality Agency and the reports by the Male Champions of Change, there are now many collection points. The case for measurement, it seems, has been legitimised.

Data alone is not the answer, of course. It's necessary, but reporting and publication of gender statistics is not sufficient. However, without clear evidence of what is or is not improving, it's difficult to set goals and establish accountability for results. Many of the newer interventions outlined in this book are contingent on delivering tangible outcomes. Collecting statistics on the lack of women at executive level or pay anomalies is designed to provide a trigger for effective solutions as well as applying a bit of pressure via naming and shaming. But those who oppose targets, much less quotas, tend to fall back on excuses about corruption of standards when they are mentioned. Supporters, including many of the men quoted here, not only see the need for sustained reporting but also increasingly understand that to insist that merit will be compromised by setting targets is to defend the status quo. That's a belief that owes much to the idea that fixing women will solve the inequity problem.

And while there's much debate about the size of targets, I tend to think the aim must be to ensure about half of any cohort is women. Former prime minister Julia Gillard has often mentioned the effect of the affirmative action policy in the Australian Labor Party, which launched in 1994 with the aim of ensuring women were preselected in 35 per cent of winnable seats by 2002. Before the party took this step, women made up about 14 per cent of the national legislature in Australia and although it took a few years, the numbers did finally climb. As Gillard told an ANZ function to launch the Equal Future campaign in mid-2015, if merit is distributed equally between the sexes, then members of boards who see unequal numbers know women of merit are losing out. 'Look at any where there is less than fifty-fifty and find out why', she told the business audience. 'Women of merit are out there, so go find them, it can be done.'

When it comes to data collection, some well-known leaders have put their money where their mouth is, so to speak. Several CEOs were forthright in their defence of the detailed reporting required by WGEA when there were suggestions the Federal Government was considering watering down the regime in early 2015. Martin Parkinson, who had recently left his role as Treasury secretary, told a forum that the measures were more than red tape and 'unless organisations were made to measure their progress on gender diversity by meeting specific targets, women would not be promoted into senior roles due to an "unconscious bias"'. Treasury had set a target of 35 per cent of women to be in senior leadership positions by 2016, and a longer-term target of 40 per cent, and it also set targets for hiring, while managers needed to ensure that half of people applying for jobs were women. Data, he said, was critical to accountability. The CEO of ANZ at the time, Mike Smith, also claimed the bank considered reporting 'essential to making progress', and so did the then CEO of Citibank, Stephen Roberts.[2]

Progress is also emerging from examining the detailed data captured from organisations that employ more than 100 people, which are obliged to report to the WGEA under the *Workplace Gender Equality Act 2012*. This includes outcomes against a series of gender equality indicators, including representation of women and men in the workforce, equal remuneration, and policies and strategies to promote gender equality. The information employers contribute is part of one of the world's leading troves of information, and covers over four million employees in Australia. Gathering this information helps nudge organisations towards addressing weak spots and allocating resources where it matters most. As mentioned in chapter 4, the reporting process prompted listed logistics group Asciano (now Qube) to monitor gender pay equity and close gender pay gaps. The data found a double-digit gender pay gap among managers some years ago and the company addressed the problem by introducing gender targets in manager KPIs, and working on closing pay gaps during remuneration reviews.

And the information that is being collected, compared and reported is further scrutinised, aiming to avoid window dressing, which gives a false impression of progress. A 2016 report from KPMG on listed companies' compliance with ASX diversity recommendations noted that most companies disclosed measurable objectives for improving diversity.[3] But very few set or disclosed transparent quantitative objectives such as '30 per cent of director seats to be held by women by 2018'. And most of the measurable objectives reported involved an action, such as setting up a new process, rather than an outcome.

Those companies that disclosed clear, quantifiable objectives showed a higher level of gender diversity than those that didn't, and publicly committing to them really does drive good diversity outcomes, KPMG found. And it recommended organisations examine the Male Champions of Change approach to setting 'Targets with Teeth', which ties executive incentive payments to achieving diversity targets.

It has to be said the MCC report released in 2015 didn't show as much progress as many hoped, and there were some declines recorded at senior levels. I asked Liz Broderick how she responded to the lack of results, and she said that while there were still MCC organisations that were not improving quickly enough, the overall trend was positive. 'The MCCs are taking responsibility for change and should be held account-able. Where progress is slow they should redouble their efforts. Change is never easy. It's a journey characterised by persistence. But creating more gender-diverse organisations is not beyond our capability', she added. 'Excuses are just that.'

Targets for women in management (and on boards) are a key part of the strategy for the MCC. But there's plenty of overt and covert resistance to them. It was a tricky prospect to introduce targets in the army, and indeed the defence services more broadly, where the concept was fiercely resisted and seen as highly corrosive to effectiveness because of fears merit would not be recognised. When David Morrison implemented targets to recruit women it caused a furore and led to much muttering about the ill-advised effects of the Broderick Review into the treatment of women in the ADF. But as Morrison said, 'Actions speak louder than words. If you don't have a target, what are you aiming at?' Targets for recruiting women were a harder sell both inside the government and to the public, but did help deliver change. During his four years as chief, the number of women joining the army increased by 700 and the percentage of women in the armed services increased from 10 per cent to 12 per cent.[4] His successor, Angus Campbell, has increased the target for women in the army to 23 per cent, but has deliberately avoided putting a time frame in place, as he believes that can sometimes act as a deterrent or excuse for lack of progress (more on this in chapter 7).

Targets are doomed to fail if they are simply plonked down in front of a reluctant management group who don't support or understand the thinking behind them – and see little incentive to meet them. I asked Jane Counsel, the former head of diversity at Westpac, how she handled pushback on the need for targets, which the bank rigorously introduced under former CEO Gail Kelly. For some people there was no convincing way to argue that targets wouldn't compromise merit and that was always the challenge, she said. One way to counter this scepticism was using gender data to combat the assumption, not always stated, that the system was fine and all appointments historically had been based on merit, so surely we would have naturally seen more women in leadership roles already? It was also useful to have leaders look at the actual skills required for a role rather than previous or industry experience, as that often challenged perspectives on what was classified as 'merit'.

Even with some of the best preparation, however, there will be ways to fudge meeting targets. It's particularly tempting to ignore the spirit of the idea if you are working in an environment where people strongly believe that women lack suitability for certain jobs, and this belief goes unchallenged. The aim of targets is to build demand for and create a pipeline of female candidates, but often it doesn't work out that way. Not long after a number of the larger banks like Westpac brought in targets in around 2010, a senior female banker contacted me to describe how her phone was running off the hook with calls from recruiters. After years of suffering a gender penalty, being female was starting to work in her favour as rivals scurried to pinch as many senior women as possible to quickly reach a target. This was box-ticking on overdrive. It was good news for the small but dedicated bunch of women who had toughed it out at the top for many years, but clearly it was also a short-term response that failed to encourage executives to look more widely within their own organisations for suitable women.

Some organisations can be very creative in avoiding the spirit of a directive. In early 2016 a report by the Equality and Human Rights Commission on female board appointments in the UK found that while the top 100 listed companies had reached a 25 per cent voluntary target, a deeper look at the data showed some interesting manoeuvres from some companies. About a third of the FTSE350 companies met their obligation by shrinking the board, rather than by appointing more women. They still relied strongly on established contacts – a polite way to describe the old boys' network – to appoint directors rather than opening up the appointment process.[5]

The moral panic about targets triggering a sudden and comprehensive drop in the merit and quality of appointments remains pervasive, even though there have never been more experienced and well educated women in the workforce. This strong belief, underpinned by the deficit model, makes it much harder for the few resolute women who manage to get through job selection or promotion processes to get a fair assessment, as I examined in the last chapter. Given the quality of many male appointments I've observed for years in the workplace, this level of alarm would be funny if it weren't so damaging and tenacious.

I've written about and worked for many, many organisations and not one of them was a meritocracy, unless you truly believe merit has been disproportionately bestowed on white, middle-aged men, or that everyone is treated equally and skills are uniformly defined, recognised, valued and then rewarded in most workplaces. The cream magically rises to the top in this view: trust in the smoothly functioning meritocracy fits neatly with a strong belief that marginalised groups are just missing some of the essential ingredients to succeed in these already equitable workplaces.

But this stance is becoming harder to sustain, and senior executives who claim repeatedly that they preside over a meritocracy should really read the 2010 research about the merit paradox (cited in chapter 3). This showed that the louder the declarations about how meritocratic a workplace was, the more biased towards men the outcomes were.[6] Resting on your 'meritocracy' laurels means you are more likely to avoid checking your biases, which can then flourish, the research found.

Consistent and rigorous data collection and reporting helps to counter the merit argument against targets. But statistics alone can't deliver change, and there do need to be repercussions if targets are not met, as many of the MCC group have now discovered. Targets, and quotas for women, need to come with accountability and some form of enforcement to boost the number of women making it to the top, according to the co-author of a 2015 study on the topic, professor at the Australian Graduate School of Management Bob Wood, who also runs the Centre for Ethical Leadership. Creating a significant change in the low level of women in leadership, such as on boards and in parliament, requires targets with accountability, and reporting regimes were necessary but not sufficient on their own, the international study revealed.[7] There was just no evidence that requiring companies and parliamentary bodies to report on gender diversity and publishing the resulting statistics has any impact on the election of women to company directorships or seats in parliament. However, targets and quotas with transparency and accountability do make a difference.

Setting higher goals for female representation and using stronger enforcement mechanisms, both in boards of directors and in government bodies, leads to higher representation, the study found after examining global efforts. But there were some variations in different countries. A requirement to report on board diversity was related to the appointment of more US women to directorship positions in Fortune 500 companies. But this doesn't mean that the supply of women who can take up board roles has been addressed, and this will have a major impact on future results, the authors concluded. When it came to getting more women in legislative bodies, gender targets and quotas were clearly associated with higher numbers of women on boards and in parliaments across the world – with Finland, France, Iceland, Italy, Norway (see page 117) and Sweden having either targets or quotas and reaching better levels than the world average.

Importantly, increasing the number of women in leadership positions still requires a combination of strategies on both the demand side and the supply side, the study pointed out. It recommended that 'countries, companies, and political parties seeking to increase female representation should consider quotas or targets with strong enforcement mechanisms and be mindful of the fact that, as in most areas of endeavor, the level of representation achieved will be directly related to the level of challenge in the goal set and how much the goal has been accepted by the key stakeholders.'

Enforcement mechanisms around pay tend to grab the attention of executives. Some of the work done by MCC organisations has focused on restructuring pay and rewards systems to make sure there are repercussions from failing to meet targets. The old saying, 'What gets measured gets managed', is often used but there's another equally pertinent adage: 'What gets rewarded gets repeated'. Sustained efforts to balance the gender equation are not likely to be taken seriously until there are repercussions from failure – and setting up the rules differently decreases the risk that these efforts can slip off the agenda when an enthusiastic supporter moves on. At Goldman Sachs Australia, senior executives have a key performance indicator on diversity and are measured against how well they have made progress. The same approach was used at the ASX, with former CEO Elmer Funke Kupper setting what he described as 'stretch' targets in 2013, of 40 per cent women at all levels, with the performance of executives against this measure accounting for 20 per cent of their bonuses.

While many in the business sector are still squeamish about stronger enforcement measures, and feel enough has been done, it has been a struggle to increase the number of female directors (and management ranks are even harder to crack) to anywhere near the 39 per cent currently on Australian government boards. In 2016, as noted, the AICD announced a target of 30 per cent women on boards by 2018, and the chair Elizabeth Proust didn't shy away from suggesting quotas could be considered at some stage if progress remained sluggish. Perhaps another means of boosting the number of female directors would be to appoint more women as chairs, with recent analysis showing companies with female chairs have more diverse groups of directors. But women chair just 4.8 per cent or 24 companies in the ASX500, according to gender researcher Conrad Liveris.[8] Liveris also used ASX data to track the gender of chairs and directors and found that companies with female chairs have more female directors than those with men at the helm. (Research published in the *Financial Times* found the same dynamic in the UK.[9]) A handful of Australian companies had 50 per cent or more female directors (Medibank Private, Woolworths, AMP, Mirvac, Boral and Nine Entertainment) according to AICD data released in 2016.[10] AMP and Medibank have female chairs, and Mirvac a female CEO. Seems the idea that women in power are naturally prone to sabotaging other women's careers might be a furphy.

Ambitious targets are also being used at state government level, where there has been a more energetic approach to the dilemma. The Tasmanian government has announced a 50 per cent target for women on boards by 2020, and the same goal has been set by the Victorian Government. It's a good start, according to Australian Sex Discrimination Commissioner Kate Jenkins, who was asked at the National Press Club if the government was taking gender equality seriously, following her first public appearance in 2016. There were good examples of change, she said: 'In Victoria there was an announcement that on all government boards, fifty per cent of appointments would be women. The secretary of one of the departments, who was responsible for the water board, said, "Well, if we do that, we'll take a long time to get there", so he spilled all the water boards, and he appointed fifty per cent men, fifty per cent women. And from my point of view, there were a lot of various views about that approach, but actually that's disruptive change'. Despite dire warnings, the outcome was not terrible and the boards appointed terrific women, she pointed out, but it takes courage and leadership to make these changes.

As we've seen, critics of affirmative action of all kinds and quotas in particular have been using the 'merit' arguments against these measures for so many years that it in some cases it has become self-fulfilling, as academic neuropsychologist and author Cordelia Fine points out.[11] 'One of the most common objections to quotas [...] is that they violate the principle of merit. This objection of course implies that if sufficient numbers of able, competent and successful women existed for the roles, then they would most certainly already have them. Such confidence in a level playing field for the sexes has a surprisingly long history.' And even today, it is clear that merit is a subjective concept, she points out. Bias is often the culprit, even if it is implicit rather than overt. But affirmative action, like quotas, can mess with the minds of the women who are recipients of these programs, particularly in workplaces where women are facing scepticism about their credentials for a job.

'Several studies, many led by New York University's Madeline Heilman, a professor of psychology, have confirmed that female employees hired under affirmative action are regarded as less competent than, say, identically qualified men. Female beneficiaries, in turn, make similar inferences about themselves. Particularly, in the absence of feedback to the contrary, their own self-beliefs and behaviour follow suit, leading to lower self-ratings of confidence, a timid, performance-limiting approach to work and a diminished interest in continuing in leadership positions.' As Fine points out, even if there are qualified women for boards or indeed senior management appointments, should they work in a culture that thinks rather differently about their suitability, then 'affirmative action may have undermining, self-fulfilling psychological effects'.

That's why the ridiculously popular notion that women are born lacking the confidence gene, as I examine in chapter 8, thrives. But it's a misreading of cause and effect – it's behaviour in the workplace, not the female chromosomes that are usually to blame. And other factors may be playing a role when it comes to confidence. There is a growing awareness in the Australian business community that domestic violence has a significant impact on workplaces. Intimate partner abuse, which is experienced by an estimated one in four women according to domestic violence prevention group Our Watch, can result in major erosion of confidence as well as serious physical injuries.[12]

The perceptions about women appointed under affirmative action programs or to comply with targets reveal a complex picture, and can be a deterrent. The CEO of Australia Post, Ahmed Fahour, has concerns about repercussions from targets and using incentives and penalties for something that obviously needs to be done. However, Australia Post, which has nearly 40 per cent of women in management and 38 per cent on its executive committee, does measure and report on its gender diversity and achievements annually. 'I think we should be demanding every corporation has some kind of "gender gap" analysis, whether it's pay or jobs, and to be held publicly to account on those', he said.[13]

Fortunately, it's getting harder to ignore the evidence that merit and targets can co-exist and indeed, at times, even result in improved quality of boards and senior executive groups. The Norwegian evidence makes this clear (see page 117), where it's evident that having more women on boards improves their quality. A range of studies show that increased diversity leads to higher performance – not because women are better than men (or people of colour better than white people) but because they can bring different experience to the role, and are often appointed by organisations with more considered recruitment practices and a stronger interest in qualifications regardless of gender or race.[14]

And the public are becoming far less willing to tolerate excuses when low levels of women are blamed on lack of merit. Many Australians will recall the day newly elected prime minister Tony Abbott announced his first cabinet in 2014, in which there was one woman appointed out of the 18 ministers – Foreign Minister Julie Bishop. Asked about the glaring omission, the prime minister said he was disappointed (in the inadequacy of women, presumably) but that the appointments were based on merit. He assured a stunned populace that there were women 'knocking on the door' of cabinet in the outer ministry. His predecessor Julia Gillard had seven women in her cabinet but presumably different door-opening criteria.

It was intriguing to note that in 2016, in an overdue *mea culpa* from the deposed Abbott – whose own party replaced him with Malcolm Turnbull – he mentioned this failure to appoint women to his cabinet as a reason for his downfall. Turnbull apparently had different ideas about merit, because he immediately rustled up five women for his first cabinet, and subsequently declared himself a feminist. It wasn't quite a Justin Trudeau moment (who had appointed 50:50 women and men in his first cabinet after he was elected as Canadian Prime Minister in 2015), but it was an improvement. Unfortunately, following the 2016 election, while the number of women in the House of Representatives increased overall, there were just 13 women on the government benches, igniting calls for a quota in the Liberal and National Party Coalition. At least this outcry, and that over the lopsided Abbott cabinet, revealed that a broad swathe of society objected to such old-fashioned attitudes. It was, however, cold comfort at the time.

Despite what happens in our minds that leaves us questioning the ability of a woman when she is appointed under a target, a process Fine explained so well, the resistance to quotas appears to be shifting. I've heard many women strongly object to the concept over the years but a few have recently changed their tune in the face of glacial progress. Half of a large cohort of international female company directors surveyed in 2016 supported quotas in the boardroom, but less than 10 per cent of their male colleagues agreed.[15] Female directors, the same study revealed, were also more likely than men to approve of term limits and mandatory retirement ages to change corporate board membership. I wasn't surprised to read about these results.

One of the contributing groups to the report was the Women Corporate Directors (WCD) Foundation (along with Harvard Business School and Spencer Stuart). In 2014 I sat in a conference hall in Paris at the Global Summit of Women, organised by WCD, and watched the hands shoot up when the 600 or so women from around the world in the room were asked if they supported mandatory measures to increase numbers of women. We were in the right place at the right time to discuss this, as France introduced legislated quotas of 40 per cent women for the top 40 listed companies in 2011, with companies given until 2017 to comply. At the time of the conference, there were 30 per cent women on top boards, up from 8 per cent in 2006. The current level is 35 per cent. While the process was not without problems, the French businesswomen I spoke to said there had been very little chance of any significant change without the new law. And the business sector was adjusting.

Which makes me wonder just how realistic the concerns and warnings are about falling standards and the divisiveness of quotas in the business world? I got a message in 2016 from an Australian businesswoman I know who had just returned from a trip to South Africa. She had seen the way the legislated Black Economics Empowerment (BEE) requirements were being tackled by business and found it 'fascinating'. The BEE gives preferential treatment to historically disadvantaged groups through employment preference, skills development and preferential procurement. While not everyone agreed with the legislation content, and it was time consuming, by and large most people see the advantage of it, and discussions and the implementation work is filtering down through businesses, she explained. 'They are getting on with it without too much fuss, the roof has not caved in. It was eye opening with all the hand wringing that goes on over here (in Australia) about quotas.'

The evidence about the impact of quotas right around the world poses a challenge to those who would dismiss quotas as unmitigated failures or only suitable for Nordic social democracies. It suggests they deliver results quickly when many other options have failed. To attack board quotas for failing to increase the number of women in management ranks could be to miss the point. Maybe the results to date prove the case for using mandated quotas in management ranks too, rather than showing that they are untenable? After all, targets for women have now been adopted by many organisations, and technically it's not a major change to tighten up the framework by adding repercussions for non-compliance.

But of course, important as measurement and targets are, they need to be accompanied by behavioural change, as Deborah Gillis, the CEO of US-based women and work research firm Catalyst, told me when she visited Australia in 2015. The reporting data collected by WGEA, and the formation of the Male Champions of Change, were examples of steps ahead but there were still deeply entrenched cultural dynamics to shift here and in other countries, she said. And having just one woman on a board or in a government cabinet really stands out. 'One is the new zero – it's socially unacceptable to have no women on a board so you go and find one and then say, "We're done".'

When robust gender data is published and targets are set in many businesses, it quickly exposes tokenism in appointing women. And it highlights the folly of believing the system will just rectify itself or that merit has been compromised by these steps. It's true quotas and targets are not subtle instruments, and they offend many of us because we think of ourselves as fundamentally fair. And there are many more refinements needed so that the principle of the approach is observed rather than short-term compliance. But the great boon of having so much data available is that it makes it much harder to argue that gender imbalance is simply the result of inherent deficiencies, or individual choices about jobs and caring. This allows a clearer view of the structural culprits and solutions, which will continue to change over time. So will the use of targets and quotas: they are circuit breakers and stepping stones to change, which should ultimately be redundant once a better gender balance is reached.

The more strident objections to mandatory measures rely heavily on a belief many women who lack merit would be appointed because they simply don't have a lot of it to start with, unlike men. But this emphasis on the supply-side problem also needs adjusting, and targets create demand for women, which over time allows a pipeline to be established. Meanwhile, some of the energy and attention currently being poured into objections to quotas and warnings about merit could actually be well directed to analysing a range of existing and puzzlingly popular diversity programs in many workplaces – which have failed to deliver much progress while reinforcing the deficit approach.

A NORWEGIAN STORY

I've followed the debate about quotas and the Norwegian experience with great interest over many years. Examining the story reveals how many of the well-worn arguments are distracting and inaccurate, because they revolve around a perceived lack of quality on the supply side of the women on boards equation. The quota law in Norway came into effect from 2008, and means the state can dissolve firms that do not comply, which unleashed anguished howls of outrage from business leaders – and some women, too. The sentiment has been shared by many other business cohorts around the world: in fact, the stock response in Australia or the UK to Norway's plunge into legislated quotas is to label the entire program a failure. Actually, that is far from the case, as several academic studies have found.

A core objection to the quota (often heard about targets) was a dearth of qualified female candidates, or women with an appetite for the roles, in Norway's small economy. In fact, if the qualifications required were narrow and hinged on past CEO experience, as analysis from 2016 notes, the playing field was indeed very narrow, as there simply weren't many former female CEOs.[16] But in practice, the new obligations motivated a different approach to the search. 'Nomination committees and owners were forced to broaden the criteria, and many new and interesting board candidates appeared, including younger female specialists, in technology, finance, law or some other field highly relevant to companies' strategy. This has even broadened the board recruitment field for men, as more young men with international and entrepreneurial backgrounds appear on boards now. Another important effect of the gender balance law is that it has resulted in diversity beyond gender to include different backgrounds, education and experience.'[17] A number of findings on the Norwegian model have shown that female directors on average have better educational credentials than male directors.

The quota law has also had a broader social effect by redistributing power in Norwegian society, according to academic Aaron Dhir, who interviewed a range of directors about their experience.[18] It forced companies to extend their searches for new directors beyond the usual spheres. 'As a result, Norwegian society's understanding of high-level leadership is changing, valuing a wider variety of backgrounds and experiences.'[19] The heterogeneity in the boardroom improved the quality of deliberations and corporate governance, his studies revealed. While there were many reasons why the US, for example, was unlikely to entertain the idea of quotas, Dhir points out voluntary measures have not been very effective and it is clear that a more forceful regulatory shove is needed to disrupt the status quo.

Quotas haven't automatically resulted in more women being appointed to top management ranks in Norway, but there has been a slow improvement. In 2003, 30 per cent of working women in Norway were employed in roles categorised as managers and by 2015, the number rose to 37 per cent.[20] While greater progress would be ideal, this is still an improvement that is often ignored in the rush to label Norway's approach a disaster. In fact, the dire warning that the business sector would simply not abide by quotas has not only been proven wrong, but the experience has even produced some male evangelists. Casting the net more widely for directors and using formal selection processes has been a welcome spin-off from the quota legislation, according to the chair of Norway's Statoil, Svein Rennemo.[21] The tendency in the past to put a bunch of grumpy old male CEOs on boards was not a good model, he said, and the process for appointing directors was now more professional. In fact, Norway should export the election committee model because it forces through a professional process, he explained.

And it's not just Norway that has taken the plunge, as Italy, Belgium, France, Iceland, and Germany have also introduced quotas that require corporate boards to maintain particular levels of gender balance. Malaysia, India and Brazil also use different forms of quotas. Although the resistance from business sectors in countries such as the US, UK and Australia has been driven by catastrophising about the lack of suitable women, the reality is that legislated quotas are not about to make an appearance any time soon. But the experience in Norway and other countries debunks many myths about quotas and offers some potent lessons for recognising there are plenty of skilled candidates when gender becomes an advantage rather than a deficit.

CHAPTER 6

Promotions not panaceas

'Mentors talk with you, sponsors
talk about you.'

HEATHER FOUST-CUMMINGS,
CATALYST'S SENIOR DIRECTOR OF RESEARCH

MANY OF US KNOW WHAT it's like. There's a meeting to get to but the
timing means a dash home straight afterwards, and that means
there will be bags to carry, possibly shopping for dinner, gym
gear or even that craft stuff you need for the kids' school concert
costume. The burden of fitting together the demands of paid
and unpaid work at home still often sits on women's shoulders.
And so it was that a busy woman hurried to her meeting with

a senior male mentor who had recently been assigned to her to help her with career advice.

She was carrying some shopping as she raced to meet her mentor and was looking forward to spending some time discussing how to better navigate the corporate world. What she didn't expect was a ticking-off from this senior executive, who wasted little time in telling her that bringing shopping to a meeting was highly unprofessional. In his opinion. It's a story that did the rounds of the women's business community in Sydney when a high-profile professional body decided to launch, with much fanfare, a mentoring scheme to help more women get into senior ranks. Neither the mentors nor those being mentored had much preparation, and often enough, the senior men involved had very little idea of the problems and career concerns the women were facing.

It's not so much a gender gap in experience as a yawning chasm. Another anecdote that circulated at the same time concerned the head of this same professional body ringing up one of Australia's highest-profile female directors about the mentoring program. She assumed, understandably given her stature and experience, that she was being approached to act as a mentor. She was wrong: it was an invitation to be mentored, even though she had far more experience than the man inviting her. When she declined, she was told it didn't really matter as her participation was just 'to tick a box'.

Not all mentoring schemes for women are so flawed. There's been a boom in demand for these programs but a surprising lack of scrutiny on how they are structured and whether they actually deliver. And the invitation list is usually exclusive: 'high-potential' women or a small senior group, who get to join either internal schemes matching senior executives with more junior women, or are sent off to mentoring programs run by consulting firms. But if the aim has been to get more women through the ranks, there's not much to show for it. If anything, the progress of women into senior ranks has been as glacial as ever – or has gone backwards – in recent years. That can't be blamed on mentoring alone, of course, but many organisations are simply not able to point to a tangible link between mentoring and better results. Perhaps it's because these relationships end up focusing once again on fixing women and as Sheryl Sandberg suggests, are more like a form of therapy.

But I have an important qualification to make here. Whenever I talk about this topic at least one anguished woman or man will ask me why I hate mentoring. I don't. Of course I have been mentored, and have mentored others. It is a key part of learning and becoming more effective, no matter what your job or gender. And I have had just as many terrific male mentors as female ones over my career. What I am challenging is the use of specific mentoring schemes for senior women that promise to help them advance through traditional gender barriers, and over-reliance on this as a corporate panacea for much more structural problems. Just to be clear.

The amount of research pointing to flaws in mentoring and other diversity programs (more on these soon) which aim to educate employees and managers on how bias operates is gathering pace. While these may be a good first step in raising awareness of gender and other biases, on their own they can be ineffective in countering biases that taint decisions in organisations, a US study found.[1] Mentoring and networking programs also didn't help much to increase diversity and were aimed more at addressing social isolation, Harvard Business School professor Francesca Gino concluded. Interestingly, research cited by Gino found the key to increasing the number of women in leadership was to have accountability for diversity, such as through committees or a diversity manager.

There are a few other favourite corporate remedial responses to pesky gender problems. In late 2015, I attended a workshop arranged by consultants Margaret Byrne and Grant Robertson with a group of diversity experts and heads from some of Australia's largest companies. We came up with a list of common diversity activities that were proving unhelpful.[2]

- *Mentoring, especially in-house 'vanilla mentoring'* has largely failed to deliver change. Instead, 'sponsorship' (more on this soon) is viewed as being much more likely to progress gender balance.

- *General unconscious bias training*, research shows, might have done more harm than good. Like the assertiveness training that it succeeded, it may have a few niche applications (for example, identifying systemic bias) but is pretty much discredited as a general approach to achieving gender balance.

- *Diversity councils* can be useful. But many have a 'hands-off' approach, leaving the heavy lifting to a company's human resources department. This results in the rest of the organisation investing far less energy in attracting and keeping employees from diverse backgrounds. For some organisations, diversity councils are little more than window dressing.

- *Extraordinary role models* such as high-flying female leaders don't much help the 'average' person. Additionally, context is critical, so lessons and tips from these stars can't be easily replicated.

Using just one approach is not helpful in addressing diversity issues, our discussion found. But many managers in this field still focus on mentoring and unconscious bias awareness, and see them as the 'silver bullet' for gender balance.

Australian academic and consultant Dr Jennifer de Vries has analysed the practice of mentoring and found it was currently seen as a 'panacea for a variety of organisational ills'. Despite looking like an ideal way of addressing career problems, these women-only programs tend to overpromise and underdeliver.[3] The failure to hit the mark is partly an issue of a maturing understanding of what causes gender barriers: when it seemed that the problem lay with women and their lack of skill, then mentoring looked like a sensible option, although never a solution on its own. But now there is a much better picture of the ingredients that make up discrimination over an entire working life, as de Vries points out, with strong evidence about the cumulative disadvantage women face over many years, and not just when their noses are pressed against the glass ceiling.

A plethora of mentoring programs focus on personal adjustments to women and not the structures they work in, which gender and organisation scholars argue is fundamentally misguided, de Vries says. Instead of seeing women as being in need of help, these researchers believe, it's the jungle they work in that needs transforming.[4] Mentoring is about a short agenda with a focus on individuals, compared to the much harder and longer agenda of tackling who has power and how that reproduces inequality.

In practice, the traditional pairing of an older, powerful man with a less experienced woman can send a troubling message, possibly unintentional but potent anyway, to women throughout the ranks. It's all about experienced men handing out advice as though they have the keys to the kingdom and women need to get information from an expert. This isn't exactly reinforcing female empowerment. That's a byproduct familiar to the former head of diversity at Citigroup, NAB, and King and Wood Mallesons, Neil Cockcroft, who has observed many corporate mentoring schemes for women. He also spent many years in an archetypally masculine workplace, the British Army. After working in Australia for several years, Cockcroft returned to live and work as a diversity specialist consultant in London, where we caught up in 2016. The inequality challenges in the UK are similar to those in Australia, he said, and as our understanding develops of the effect of diversity initiatives over time – including the unintended consequences – there's a strengthening case to re-examine the impact of mentoring.

Senior male mentoring without more active sponsorship may have a limited impact on accelerating women's careers. Secondly, mentoring may be based on a deficit model to equip women with skills they are assumed to be lacking. Needless to say, mentoring doesn't challenge the male model and helps prop up the existing norms for what it takes to be successful, he added. 'The irony is that mentoring schemes may therefore reinforce traditional, male-dominated power structures and "in-groups", rather than transforming them.' A lack of measurable changes or results from mentoring can also lead to disillusionment, he noted.

Some new versions, such as reverse mentoring, take a different tack when junior women enlighten senior men about the realities of their experience. In the UK, professional services firm EY introduced a reverse mentoring scheme designed to be used alongside other initiatives to help shift sexist attitudes.[5] No doubt this will deliver some penny-dropping moments. And while it is no remedy in itself, if it helps ignite an interest in confronting sexism among influential male executives and identifies the depth of talented younger women in an organisation who might otherwise go unnoticed, then it has value.

Despite some serious flaws in the way women are traditionally mentored, even the critics believe there is an upside to redesigning programs or introducing something called sponsorship, where there is a focus is on actively promoting women. Moving the focus away from potentially fixing women to finding actual opportunities for them is an important distinction. New formats, such as the reverse mentoring I've mentioned, group or peer mentoring, or workshops to create networks of men and women can be of real help to individuals and in changing the workplace, according to de Vries.

A few organisations are starting to modify the standard women's mentoring model. Lance Hockridge, while CEO of transport company Aurizon, had a program that wasn't mentoring per se but rotates women in management ranks into a job in the CEO's office for a few months. It helps give them some more detailed understanding of line management roles. He's not sure that the traditional mentoring programs, which have proved so popular in many corporates – designed to lift middle management women up the ladder – have had much impact on the numbers of women in top ranks. But he says there's a complex range of reasons why.

'Some of it's tokenism and it's actually about sheer hard work and this is confronting stuff. It's time consuming and not inexpensive. These mentoring programs don't work when they plonk someone who works with someone for six months and will then transfer – it's doomed to failure. It's not being clear about goals either.' The outcome should be about knowledge acquisition, and women often find it difficult to spend a period in a mentoring program when no clear performance indicators are set, he adds.

There's been very clear feedback from women on the topic of mentoring at Goldman Sachs Australia, says CEO Simon Rothery. 'They are over mentoring and want sponsorship. All my female direct reports were sponsored. And we ask managers where they are with the women in their groups, if they leave, where have they gone and why. It leads to more results.' Now that sponsorship is the name of the game, a few companies are altering their former approach and changing mentoring programs to something more directed to concrete outcomes. In 2015 UK media company Sky launched a Women in Leadership program to boost the proportion of women in its top 500 jobs – broadly those within three levels of the chief executive – from one-third to half.[6] Part of the initiative was a sponsorship program 'where executive teams will select women from their area to be paired with a senior figure, with the clear understanding that once they have mapped out strengths and ambitions, it is then their job to go out and advocate for the individual'. Sponsorship programs, however, also need to be designed rather than simply dumped in the lap of a busy executive.

Other efforts to tackle gender bias have also come under analysis recently. Reducing managerial bias through diversity training and evaluations were the least effective methods of increasing the proportion of women in management, according to research.[7] And there are three main reasons why some of these training and unconscious bias awareness programs appear to fail, according to research by Frank Dobbin and Alexandra Kalev: it reinforces stereotypes and heightens bias, it fosters complacency, and it makes whites feel excluded.[8] The fact that most diversity programs aren't increasing diversity shouldn't come as a surprise, according to further research from 2016.[9] The bulk of these approaches are unchanged from the 1960s and were designed to head off legal action on discrimination by policing managers' thoughts and actions. The problem is that 'force-feeding can activate bias rather than stamp it out', according to the Dobbin and Kalev study. The positive effects of diversity training rarely last beyond a day or two, according to the researchers, but nearly half of midsize companies use it, as do nearly all the Fortune 500.

Not surprisingly, given the increase in scrutiny, when Facebook launched a series of online bias training programs for employees in 2015, it was greeted with some scepticism by commentators.[10] 'There's just one problem: bias training usually fails to increase workplace diversity. Raising awareness of bias, which Facebook's lectures aim to do, can even strengthen it. Companies often spend millions on poorly designed training. When designed well, training can be one useful tool among other diversity initiatives such as assigning responsibility for diversity to special managers. But Facebook has released no data on whether its Managing Unconscious Bias course actually works.'[11]

Although this kind of unconscious bias training is often introduced with the best intentions, the results have been difficult to track, and it's estimated that between US$6–8 billion a year is spent in the US alone on unconscious bias and diversity training. According to the *Wall St Journal*, in 2014 about 20 per cent of US companies were offering this kind of training but the ratio was expected to rise to 50 per cent. That's an awful lot of expensive and time-consuming programs.[12]

So what is the problem with alerting people to their biases? I have certainly seen first hand the benefit of educating sceptics about the causes and dimensions of gender bias in workplaces and am not a fan of throwing the baby out with the bathwater when it comes to these efforts. But sometimes there can be a gap between theory and practice, or unintended consequences. While it may sound like a contradiction, some of the business efforts in this area may actually normalise bias by leading people to think it is simply a failing that everyone has and so can't be helped. The problem is complicated, according to academic Melissa Thomas-Hunt.[13] Most people don't intentionally stereotype because bias may be operating outside their awareness, so we need to be motivated to counter it and that means we need to be aware of it. But you can't expect managers, executives and employees to police their own biases, and Thomas-Hunt says leaders have to structure processes correctly to weed it out. 'Organizations need to put into place certain standardized processes that give managers less discretion in how we evaluate people. It takes full-time concentration to fight bias on our own. That's unrealistic.'

If interview questions for hiring an employee are designed to specifically assess skills and are uniformly asked of all job candidates, then bias will be minimised, she says. A more diffi-cult situation to tackle would be assessing employees, which is often done through informal 'micro-assessments of individuals' based on numerous daily encounters. In that situation, in which bias can easily sneak in, Thomas-Hunt suggests that managers be required to assess employees in a much more structured way by writing down notes on performance every so often.

This whole topic of unconscious bias is a fairly tricky and not well understood issue, says Australian psychologist and founder of organisational consulting firm Psynapse, Jennifer Whelan, who regularly writes and runs workshops on workplace diversity, inclusion and innovation. At the 'All About Women' conference in Sydney in early 2016, I ran a sold-out session with Whelan as she explained some of the background on bias and brain func-tion. The study in the article by Thomas-Hunt is about the social dynamics of legitimising bias, Whelan says. If we believe bias is common, we are less motivated to do anything about it because it is seen as normal. Unfortunately there is truth in this belief: every brain operates in ways that produce predictable biases, and stereotyping (unconscious and conscious) is actually fairly pervasive.

We later discussed how the appetite for unconscious bias training has grown as it became a favoured means of address-ing the need for better diversity. But even though Whelan runs workshops that cover these areas for a range of organisations, she has some reservations about the motivation and expecta-tions of some employers who may want to tick a box, or check off a commitment made by their executive team, she said. But less cynically, some really do hope that awareness will lessen the impacts of bias on hiring decisions – and they also hope that somehow you'll be able to pull a rabbit out of a hat and give them the secret antidote to unconscious bias. 'There isn't one, of course – the strategies for minimising the effects of bias only work if they are actually practised and carried out. Day-to-day life and the pace of work typically get in the way of leaders actually doing things differently, though', she explained.

The first wave of unconscious bias work crested a couple of years ago, according to Whelan, but over 2015 and 2016 there was renewed interest. One factor is that it's still a 'sexy' concept, or intriguing for most people, and Whelan also thinks many organisations still believe that 'it's a silver bullet of sorts, even though experience tells us that unless it is integrated with inclusion work, it won't do much on its own. It's also a nice, "self-contained", single-issue intervention that can be done easily in a one-off process'. The topic of bias is important and Whelan believes it needs to be included in the diversity agenda. But she doesn't think it's the 'be all and end all', nor a cure on its own, and it should sit inside a more comprehensive program of work around inclusion.

While every organisation would like to know if it makes a difference, Whelan said none that she has worked with are actually prepared to measure this properly, which would involve measuring recruitment and promotions decisions both before and after training. 'We are currently working with two clients, though, who have inclusion metrics embedded in their engagement surveys, and intend to track changes after an inclusive leadership training program we are implementing. This is a reasonable start to trying to track impact.'

The effectiveness of this training can depend on a classic misperception in organisations that no-one is consciously biased, so dealing with the unconscious variety will cure the problem. But as Whelan explains, the reality is that most organisations don't really want to believe that they have plenty of consciously sexist, prejudiced or bigoted leaders in their ranks – or people who simply don't believe more social equality is needed. And, sadly, no amount of training will have an impact on these people.

Having worked on a number of reviews on gender for the public sector, consultant Deborah May (whose Treasury review is detailed in chapter 1) has seen a lot of interest in unconscious bias programs but believes they must be approached with care. 'It's not just about recognising bias but asking "How does it get in the way?" The unconscious bias training in the typical way it is delivered is not helpful. The bias is around systems and processes', she told me. Workshops about how bias operates in our brains can be a bit too directed at the individual and may not get the message across about what can be done to make rules and practices work better for everyone.

Given the evidence that's accumulating, it will be interesting to see if the efficacy of unconscious bias training warrants some more attention in the future. I suspect the organisational love affair is not about to die. It has some hallmarks of a panacea but at least it involves both men and women. And with more focus on how to take steps to interrupt bias and measure change it may prove more effective. That can't be said of another popular fall-back in the list of not particularly helpful organisational diversity responses: the focus on sanctifying over-achieving women.

This pedestal positioning sets up impossibly high standards by focusing on over-achievers, who can seem way out of the orbit of women in much more lowly jobs. I think it's important to point out that role models are needed and the old saying 'You can't be what you can't see' has more than a grain of truth in it. We do need to see women in all kinds of jobs, and running businesses, to make such achievements seem normal and possible.

But it also seems to me that putting a halo around super-achieving women with a brood of children and a high-level career is actually, perversely, part of the deficit model at work too. The implication is that 'having it all' is a reasonable goal and that women who find the going tough are missing the right stuff to be good mothers and serious workers. It puts the onus squarely back on their shoulders to suck it up and get on with the double shift, while managing contradictory expectations about being competent and caring. And on top of all that, they are often expected to prove they have merit on a daily basis. Phew. (My friend Jane Caro says men are assumed to have merit until proven otherwise and women are assumed not to have merit until proven otherwise.)

The glowing portrayals of successful women almost always include some family management details that are missing in portraits of successful men. This is not helpful and, worse, it reinforces those double standards that need to be eradicated. I suspect our appetite for lessons from high achievers (no matter how banal their advice) is not about to go away. But until more women are spread through more sectors and jobs at all levels, there will be a tendency to highlight those who doggedly made it to the pinnacle. They are, of course, incredibly capable and resilient and they deserve to be admired. But they are very unusual. We'll know we have had some success in this struggle when women don't have to be better than their peers at everything.

It reminds me of the old description of Ginger Rogers: she did everything as well as Fred Astaire did but backwards and in high heels. It's great to be inspired but when the bar is set too high and the difficulties are downplayed, it can have the opposite effect.

The point of analysing much of the current suite of organisational diversity options is not to throw the good out with the bad – nor to put the onus on women to sit through more training and take responsibility for delivering results. Organisations with more effective approaches tend to try a lot of programs, measure their effect and then alter policies and practices. And they include everyone. I'm all for trying out a range of different approaches, as many of the successful examples in this book show. But doing the same thing over and over again and expecting a different outcome is a much-quoted definition of madness. Often enough, a response that had some success in the past doesn't deliver in different circumstances. A challenge to the orthodox response to diversity in many organisations is overdue, particularly as serious interest in gender inequality from the top is on the increase. After all, most other business strategies that fail to deliver are routinely and critically examined and altered.

My experience also suggests there's a key distinction between remedial approaches and the rest. I'm a fan of forums run by and for women to discuss and address the bias they encounter. As a regular speaker at these events, I have repeatedly seen the value of these safe environments for discussing and comparing experience. (Strangely enough, given the imbalance of power between female employees and male leaders, I'd say the Male Champions of Change has operated in much the same way for the men in the group. Many are used to being in control and all over the facts, but need to ask and learn a lot about this issue and acknowledge mistakes.)

I'm often told by women who turn up, sometimes reluctantly, to these forums that the conversation has helped contextualise what is happening to them in the workplace. Many find that hearing from others and about the big picture and research on discrimination, rather than being lectured on what they are doing wrong, can depersonalise the sexism they face. It can help them drop the guilt, and challenge bias and snide comments more effectively. Let's face it, it would be far better if these seminars (and the MCC) were redundant, but we are a long way from an even playing field. Until then, these events meet a real need. Even being in a room full of women can be affirming, and on the practical side I've watched strong bonds and alliances form on many occasions. That can make all the difference when you are facing tough conditions or toxic attitudes.

But we shouldn't expect these women's networks to also have an impact on powerful men. The 2016 report by the UK's Equality and Human Rights Commission (EHRC) revealed very slow progress getting women on boards and showed the old boys' network was still alive and kicking, according to writer and activist Laura Bates. And women's networks were not going to make much difference. 'Part of the problem is that it tends to be mainly women who are involved in diversity projects and mentoring networks, while men at the top are busy making the decisions that have the greatest impact. All the brilliant women's networking in the world can't help female candidates if the opportunity to reach the executive board is decided by a group of men calling on those they already know and socialise with.'

Remedial work on women, Bates says, puts the blame

squarely on women's own shoulders, suggesting many simply aren't trying hard enough, when the EHRC study reveals the real problem may lie elsewhere. 'What use is there in training a woman to negotiate fiercely and put herself forward for a senior role if the top jobs are being handed down from the mostly white, male boys' club to their mostly white, male circles of acquaintances? What use are good personal presentation skills if you never get the chance to present your candidacy because the position isn't advertised in the first place?'[14] She's spot on. But if the cosy boys' club is going to be dismantled, much more needs to be done to open up these informal power groups. Oddly enough, the chances of doing that can be bolstered by setting up a very different version of the boys' network, such as the male champions model, to help with the task.

Assessing the value of all these various choices on the diversity menu has to include a focus on organisational expectations too. When women's networks, mentoring and bias training are being trotted out as signature programs to bolster an organisation's diversity credentials, then it's time to take a closer look. One limitation of relying only on development (in any form) for women, according to Cockcroft, is that, at best, it typically grows or extends a female-centric network and that doesn't make a difference to exclusive male-dominated networks at leadership levels. The same goes for the ubiquitous diversity councils, which can attract scepticism about efficacy, given the people who sometimes sit on them. This is why organisations like Goldman Sachs have a Diversity Leadership group, made up of the top 25 most senior managing directors in the firm, which is still largely men. And it's why senior male advocates are so sorely needed.

With progress stalling and exasperation building, some of these programs don't just fail to deliver, but act as a distraction in organisations that need to get much more serious if they really want to see results. Part of the answer is to further enlist and educate more men about effective tools. And indeed, some are already homing in on the best steps to take, which are not confined to mentoring, and aim to quickly increase the attraction and retention of women – such as, strangely enough, the head of the Australian Army, as we will now see.

CHAPTER 7

Military manoeuvres: An army of women

'The standard you walk past is the standard you accept. That goes for all of us, but especially those who by their rank have a leadership role.'

FORMER CHIEF OF ARMY, DAVID MORRISON

WHEN ACTING COLONEL AMANDA FIELDING was first working in Afghanistan as a gender adviser with the Australian forces a few years ago, it wasn't unusual to run up against indifference or lack of understanding from colleagues about what her role involved – or even why she was needed there at all. She remembers the men who regularly escorted her around the region for her work

– her 'guardian angels', as they were known – slowly began to understand more about what she was doing and the plight of many women in the war-torn country.

'I travelled with a couple of Australian guardian angels [personal protection] when I travelled anywhere in Afghanistan. When I first requested support from the Australian Force Protection Team it was met with resistance, with the force protection commanders asking why it was important and what would a gender adviser do that required force protection? After they had provided protection for me on a few missions, the commanders told me that the soldiers would come back stating, "You wouldn't believe what was being talked about and what these poor women have to go through". I recall two of the soldiers on the flight coming back from Northern Afghanistan saying to me that they couldn't believe how the male forces were treating the women, nor the atrocities occurring to some of the orphaned children and asked me what we could do about it.'

The importance of the role not only became apparent to the Australian soldiers but gradually it dawned on a number of her peers within both the Australian Headquarters and the Resolute Support Mission that having women in the field was culturally important for a range of operational reasons. As Fielding recalled, in countries like Afghanistan men are unable to talk to women they do not know or search women, so at the very least a gender mix in the ranks was more than a piece of 'political correctness' and in this region, a key to the effectiveness of the security forces.

Women have been active in war zones for hundreds of years in many different roles, but it's only relatively recently, in 2012, that the Australian Defence Force (ADF) opened up the full range of combat zone positions to them. Not that this shift happened easily or quickly. The move triggered a lively discussion across not just the forces but the general community too. Dire warnings about the consequences were gravely discussed. Some of the more hair-raising predictions – that menstruating women would be picked up on enemy radar, for example, or attract sharks if they were allowed to become clearance divers – might not get as much currency these days, but still pop up occasionally during heated discussions about why women simply don't belong in the trenches.

There were always going to be objections, but the push to remove the final restrictions preventing women from serving in all ADF roles didn't simply appear on an agenda, nor was it designed to upset traditionalists, despite the impression given by the howls of outrage. It's part of a massive review of the treatment of women in the ADF that has been going on for years. And it rests on a much broader and more compelling rationale than having a few women around war zones who come in handy because they are able to speak to women in traditional Islamic communities. It's about making sure that women have the same options as men for employment and a career in the military. The fraught debate that it sparked, both in Australia and around the world, reflects the quite fundamental barriers that women face in such a classically male arena.

But facing it the ADF certainly is – and the process is fascinating, alarming and potentially revolutionary. Australia is setting some world firsts by addressing a range of barriers for women against often fierce resistance and backlash. There are plenty of unhappy men and women who think many of the moves are pointless and counterproductive. One senior woman from the forces told me in no uncertain terms that there was too much emphasis on women – which was the entire point of the exercise, after all. But she was clearly feeling the effects of some unwanted attention, generated by continuing announcements of programs to assist women. It made her intensely uncomfortable, because a great deal of the backlash has manifested in criticism and scorn about the easy ride women now get. She had been told that when it comes to jobs and promotions, it's gender rather than merit which is the main criteria for getting ahead. In fact, you could argue this has been pretty much the case for men in the military domain for centuries, but that doesn't help women facing these kinds of corrosive attitudes. No wonder they feel besieged. When you hear these objections day in and day out, there is every temptation to wish the whole focus on gender would just disappear.

And it doesn't help much in the short term to point out to capable women facing this criticism that doing nothing to address the problems for women will mean nothing changes. That women will continue to be marginalised and excluded from major training and employment opportunities, and the ADF will fall out of step with the population it defends and the rest of the world by failing to benefit from fishing in a bigger and better pond for recruits. That is the rationale behind the major reviews into women in the military. They are not just an overhaul with the potential to reframe one of the country's largest and best known employers, either, although the organisation's future capacity is definitely a major rationale. Well beyond that pretty good reason, the huge efforts being made to change such an iconically male-dominated institution are all about upending cultural norms and changing basic rules to get different outcomes. It is not about the fruitless task of moulding women into archetypal diggers or Anzacs, but modernising a national institution. This is definitely an exercise based on fixing the system and not the women.

Not everyone is happy to come along for the ride. That's because some still believe that no matter how fit or strong women are, they simply aren't diggers. And in the public imagination, as Morrison has pointed out, an Australian soldier is 'a rough-hewn country lad – invariably white – a larrikin who fights best with a hangover and who never salutes officers [...] especially the Poms'.[1] If you can't fit women into that norm, then you have to establish a new one. And while there's no underestimating the major challenges involved in doing just that, the hurdles are certainly not insurmountable, nor are all of the problems specific to Defence. But let's face it: if the Australian Army can pull this off, then surely anyone can. That's why I've particularly focused here on the efforts in this service, although the navy and airforce are also working just as hard at this and having various levels of success.

Luckily, too, the will to change is certainly evident in the very top ranks of Defence, where there's a vast to-do list and even a growing willingness to get external advice. That's why, as part of former sex discrimination commissioner Elizabeth Broderick's advice for implementing the recommendations from her major review of the treatment of women in the ADF, a Gender Equality Advisory Board (GEAB) was established in 2012. The GEAB has several external members – including me – and is jointly chaired by the Chief of the Defence Force (Mark Binskin, and previously David Hurley) and the secretary of the Department, Dennis Richardson.

It's amazing where an interest in women's rights can take you – this was not a role or organisation in which I ever expected to be involved. When I was appointed, some friends and family (a husband comes to mind) were uncharitably amused at the thought of me, a city type if ever there was one, bivouacking or on manoeuvres. As it happens, I've certainly had the last laugh – having travelled in helicopters, visited the Kapooka recruit training centre, spent a night on a large naval ship and been an observer on a major military exercise. It's been fascinating and has often challenged my own biases. And in many ways, despite the obviously daunting amount to be tackled, uplifting. Literally.

Some of the push to address women's treatment came from the now infamous Skype affair, which riveted the nation and drew attention to the ADF for all the wrong reasons. A young female cadet at the Australian Defence Force Academy was videoed, without her knowledge, having consensual sex with a male peer. One of the man's friends streamed the footage on Skype to others at the academy. The incident led to a major inquiry, with the two main perpetrators eventually leaving Defence and involved in a court case. Public outrage over the affair was loud and long. A good two years after it happened, I chatted with a young officer who had been working in the Minister of Defence's office at the time and fielded many of the calls from the public in the days after it was revealed. He was still shocked by the vehemence of the reaction; many callers were appalled at what they saw as a fundamental breach of faith in a trusted institution.

The Skype affair and another sex scandal that later emerged involving senior personnel in the army (who were known as the Jedi Council) had a galvanising effect on the senior leadership of Defence. The three service chiefs had also sat and listened to some of their own female employees describe the abuse and violence they had faced. This restorative justice process, as it is known, was arranged by Elizabeth Broderick as part of her review, and was a penny-dropping moment for them, as Morrison has recalled: 'I was sitting very uncomfortably, and with mounting disbelief, through lengthy face-to-face meetings with three women who had endured appalling physical and emotional abuse at the hands of their fellow soldiers; so much for our pride in looking after our mates. These women had been let down by their leaders and their comrades. They had been robbed of that irreplaceable component of their individual human personal identity – their dignity and self-respect. This was not the army that I had loved and thought I knew. My disbelief gave way, in turn, to shame that this had occurred in the institution to which I had devoted my entire life and of which I had been fiercely proud since I was young boy. That was my conversion experience and it had all the qualities of the road to Damascus apart from the fall from the horse.'[2]

It also motivated Morrison to record a speech that resonated around the world. The short video he delivered to his troops about the need to respect women or 'get out' of the army revealed his determination, and his exasperation with the continuing scandals and the culture they reflected.[3] No room for misunderstanding there. Acclaim for his no-nonsense calling out of poor behaviour was widespread, although plenty of those in the primary target audience – the army – were not happy about it, and were keen to tell me so when I had the chance to talk to a range of groups in the months following its delivery. They felt they were being picked on and that the incidence of sexual violence in the forces was no higher than in the general community.

But others accepted that something had to be done to stop the brutalising environment and the behaviour towards women in parts of the forces. And some saw the speech as a necessary step. Sitting around with a group of young soldiers on a joint military operation in northern Queensland in 2014, Broderick and I asked them about the speech and found that many thought the message had been overdone and was not really needed. But one young male soldier quietly disagreed. 'You just have to keep telling people this message over and over again', he said. There's no question that despite the cynicism in some quarters, the speech made it crystal-clear that the army was not just pretending to tackle this topic – it was serious. In fact, Morrison firmly believes any organisational head could deliver the same sort of clarion call to employees if they really want to – and perhaps they should.

The broadcast of that speech marked an important point for the ADF. Although a number of programs designed to attract more women into the military were already underway before the Skype affair and other scandals, the reaction to them gave a new urgency to fundamental changes and the need to be seen taking action. Public trust was eroding, recruiting targets for men and women had not been met for many years, and an urgent platform was suddenly created. The Broderick Review delivered its first report, on the Australian Defence Force Academy, in 2011, followed by a broader review in 2012.

The momentum gained from David Morrison's very tangible advocacy has helped bring public attention to the need for a new approach so women are not marginalised within the

ADF. While it won him a worldwide fan base, Morrison was still a little puzzled by the reaction, although the speech was also notable because it was written by one of the most senior transgender military officers in the world, Group Captain Cate McGregor. I asked Morrison in 2016 what he thought of its impact with the benefit of hindsight. 'I am very ambivalent about the YouTube speech. It was never intended for public consumption and it worries me that such a straightforward and unexceptional message that says, essentially, that treating your colleagues with respect is a pre-condition of your continued employment, has had the impact it has. Without doubt it got traction in the army, especially as it attracted such a large degree of public notoriety, and it served its purpose, but I don't understand its broader impact.'

It certainly marked a line in the sand for the ADF efforts, however. When Lieutenant-General Angus Campbell took over from Morrison as Chief of the Australian Army in 2015, he didn't waste time, setting out some clear goals for changing the gender equation. A former SAS commander, he grew up in a family of four boys who spent a lot of time kicking footballs around but that hasn't stopped him from a determined engagement with the agenda.

In early 2016, at the National Gallery of Australia's beautiful lecture theatre in the heart of Canberra, I heard Campbell explain his thinking on how to get more women into the resolutely masculine ranks of the army. As he spoke to an audience of women and a few men from Defence, the police, emergency and ambulance services, there was not a sound in the room. The previous presenters at this annual women's leadership summit (the National Defence, Police & Emergency Services Women's

Leadership Summit, 12 February 2016) had discussed their own careers and personal tips for success. But Campbell was on quite a different tack.

Work done by consultant Deborah May, Campbell explained, highlighted the negative aspects of how the army treats people. Women are deeply under-represented in the army, making up just 12 per cent of serving members, and it was drifting away from what the Australian community looked like, which was not a healthy thing for a democracy, nor the future of its military. A cultural reboot was needed to change the dynamics of a workplace, and the way to do it was to get the numbers right by recruiting more women to a point where the norms change: it was a classic task of changing the rules which haven't been delivering. A few months after the conference, we talked about his plans and how to tackle the inevitable resistance to gender change.

'We need to look at volume and culture. We need women to reframe the cultural messages. If I want to be in an organisation that reflects best practice, then 23 per cent women is the target. We are looking at how the system is designed to optimise each part of it but it takes twelve months to recruit someone: I describe this as structural failure. We have to fundamentally change the processes to bring in more people more quickly. We are getting further and further away from where we want to be in terms of numbers because of this structural failure. You have to set a target and looking at that analysis, we need to be getting 1050 to 1100 women joining a year to get to 23 per cent.'

'The ramifications of this system change are quite profound', he added. 'If this target for recruiting women is met then it's possible that on some courses all the trainee helicopter pilots [an army, not an airforce job], for example, could be women – we've never thought to question the courses over decades on which all trainees have been men. A balance will emerge but just recruiting from a wider talent pool is a good thing because it gives the army a wider skill set to utilise.'

'One thousand men in a valley in Afghanistan speak only to men – that's mission failure wrapped up in structural failure', Campbell stated. Even with this compelling message, he is under no illusion that some still firmly believe there is no need to rock the boat – and they assume that this focus will soon wane as everything goes 'back to normal'. But that is not an option he considers as he sets about restructuring the rules.

'I certainly don't think there's anything wrong with women, rather it is the workplace. We are not trying to change women. We have 12.2 per cent women in the army. It has grown since 2012 before which it was pretty much a flat line or about 9.9–10 per cent for decades. We've only made relatively small changes to the outcome, but what I do think we've done is a lot of the structural work that creates an environment where any person, irrespective of gender or any other factor, can serve and serve rewardingly.' Nevertheless, he admitted the army hasn't had a great sales pitch to women and the navy and air force were seeing more success, even though the structural arrangements are the same across the services, with the navy employing 19.1 per cent women and the air force 19.2 per cent, according to the 2015–16 *Women in the ADF* report.[4]

While progress will falter and some steps may work better than others, the ADF has, however, made it clear that this focus is not a passing phase of 'political correctness'. But while there are many struggles in changing the rules and recruiting processes outlined by Campbell, some of the most effective resistance comes from backlash (more on this in chapter 8). Fear and resentment build when there are challenges to a strong sense of entitlement to and ownership of roles. After all, many in the military have been at least partly attracted to their jobs because of the Anzac legend so well described by Morrison. It's an idealistic and historically masculine mystique that is all about courage, along with the physical and mental prowess needed to defend your country. So new norms for who makes a good soldier are not only about debating whether women are strong and fit enough, but whether they should be allowed to enter this domain at all. This change represents an upending and, to some, even trivialising of the semi-sacred ideal of the band of brothers or the all-male Anzacs.

This was the theme of some acute analysis of the US army and the barriers to women by Australian-based academic Megan Mackenzie.[5] At the launch of her book by former defence minister Stephen Smith in 2015, she talked about the need to tackle not just the rules but the beliefs and myths about women joining previously all-male fighting teams. The US took longer than many countries to get to the point of lifting all barriers to women, with Australia one of only about 15 countries to take the step of lifting combat exclusions (announced in 2011) and taking a five-year approach to the change, while the US followed in 2016 with its integration of women into these roles. But, as Smith pointed out, when Australia opened all combat positions to women, it didn't solve all the issues, which were about changing the culture through a range of measures.

Women are still often seen as being physically inferior to men and likely to disrupt unit cohesion and effectiveness,

MacKenzie said. Keeping women out of combat roles limits their careers and contributes to the idea that men do the real fighting, and it ignores the evidence that women have always fought. And the argument that men work better in teams without women is not backed by evidence, her analysis found. In both the US and Australia, there is a deeply held belief that women in combat roles must meet exactly the same physical standards as men. But as MacKenzie points out, physical standard tests tend to focus on upper body strength, an area where women are on average weaker than men. And there is less attention paid to abilities where women often surpass men, such as flexibility, endurance and tolerating heat. And modern warfare often involves different demands from traditional hand-to-hand combat. The ADF is also increasingly engaged in peacekeeping, such as its work in East Timor, and in rescue efforts as well as liaising with the local population in combat zones like Afghanistan.

In particular, the myth of a band of brothers – the ideal of the heroic, brave and mysterious all-male unit – is very similar to the mateship mythology in Australia's armed forces, MacKenzie explained. Australia's iconic Anzacs, as Morrison has so deftly pointed out, were exclusively male. These deeply embedded ideas about who is best suited to fight for their country have a real impact on efforts to debate, change and reform practices, particularly when it comes to the front line. 'Combat units are treated as the tip of the spear and very special', MacKenzie said at the launch. 'It's destructive because [...] myths shape policy and has shaped the debate around policy. The book shows that myths support war and make it seem clean, easy, honourable and just. Questioning the myths and assumptions and telling new stories about war, it becomes less clean, honourable and just.'

MacKenzie's work reflects growing awareness of and research into the problems for women in defence forces around the world. In Sweden the military took the unusual step of redirecting the entire budget spent on women's programs, and put it into funding education for men instead, according to research by Julie McKay, who spent three years as gender adviser to the Chief of the Defence Force and is also a member of the GEAB. As she pointed out in her report on her Churchill Fellowship study, mentoring programs, leadership training and women's networks have all been used widely by Australian businesses in a quest to 'fix' women, but there's increasing recognition that it is workplaces that need to change. Her research in business and public sectors found those which had progressed had accepted that their structure might be inherently patriarchal. Only the Swedish military had an active program focused on masculinity, the patriarchy and what might need to change to achieve gender diversity, she reported.[6]

So where has the wave of attention to this topic, particularly in the ADF, got to? As is the case in the business sphere, the actual statistics are still slow to budge, although some indicators are shifting. But there have been some notable steps forward, some around attitudes and behaviour, which can be difficult to quantify, and some important rule changes too. The Skype affair was one of the triggers for a new victim-focused approach to sexual attacks and the establishment of a Sexual Misconduct Prevention and Response Office (Sempro) by Defence – a key recommendation from the Broderick Review. Sempro has trained staff on call 24 hours to deal with complaints from men and women, and a restricted reporting regime which allows those who have been the target of attacks to get help and support without being officially identified. It is one of the few such bodies set up in a military force anywhere in the world.

As with many large private sector organisations, the forces have set clear targets for women and are reporting on progress annually in an effort to boost both recruitment and retention levels, and are crunching the numbers and what that means for the pipeline of women needed. They are also facing the fact some entire cohorts could become mainly female, which can be sobering but has not deterred General Campbell. Accountability for senior teams has also been stepped up, with the ADF introducing key performance indicators for gender inclusion to make sure decision-makers are accountable for outcomes and targets.

The forces have made some changes to ensure the basic physical requirements for recruits are structured to be fair for all, by taking into account physical differences rather than weaknesses. As Campbell explained to me, young female army recruits, for example, are given preconditioning opportunities that focus on ability, conditioning and incremental strength building rather than excessive power and dramatic improvements. The approach is seeing more men and women graduating from training at the same rate with a much reduced rate of injury.

A year or so after leaving the army, David Morrison told me the key interventions from his tenure include setting targets and naming those targets publicly, and conducting a first principles review of how they judged merit and why the existing paradigm failed to recognise the value of different, non-military life experiences. Also crucial was a series of one-on-one meetings with those affected by discrimination, harassment and bullying. 'That program began with me, and my fellow Service Chiefs but to date well over a hundred senior officers, across the Defence Force, have now met with victims to better understand the dreadful impact on individuals' self-esteem and dignity. This has been conducted under the restorative engagement process put in place by the DART (Defence Abuse Response Taskforce).'

He believes that introducing people (in almost every case women) who have great life and professional experience, but no military background, into selection panels for higher ranks has ensured a much more complete appreciation of a candidate's merit. He adds that coaching senior officers and commanding officers one-on-one to open their eyes and ears to the benefits of diversity, and putting in place more attuned recruiting campaigns that focus on the real benefits of inclusivity (such as diversity of thinking and more capable workforces) helped too. The army has also changed its rules to guarantee there would be no loss of seniority for men and women who returned to the service after a leave of absence, provided they could demonstrate their value to the long-term health of the institution.

All of these are significant steps but tell only part of the story. The harder part is finding out if behaviour and attitudes are changing as well. For some extra insights from an external adviser, I sat down with Alex Shehadie, who led the review into the treatment of women and the implementation of the Broderick Review when she worked at the Human Rights Commission (HRC). She had just left her role at the HRC (in early 2016) and joined her former colleague Elizabeth Broderick to work on a range of similar consulting projects. One of her first jobs was working with the Australian Federal Police on gender strategies:

it seems safe to say Alex clearly isn't put off by a challenge. When I asked for her assessment of real change in the ADF, she was thoughtful.

'There's been a generational shift and David Morrison speaking out helped that. There's been a shift in caring and men want to spend time with kids now – it's a change in demographics', she says. 'The more I think about it, the work around the LGBTI area has dragged the ADF into the 21st century and members of that community can march in uniform at the [gay and lesbian] Mardi Gras in Sydney now.' Perhaps most importantly, she felt the army had developed a perspective on what needed to change that concentrated on strong economic factors rather than remedial work to fit women into existing norms.

'The HRC was able to stand back as an independent body and crunch the numbers and say to them, "You are increasing your recruiting costs and nothing is changing". We were able to put it into an economic argument and to talk about the talent pool and what they were missing out on.' Fundamentally, she adds, the need to push for urgent change was coming from well beyond the military and government. 'How many more scandals are the public going to cope with?' she asks.

That's become an underlying and compelling reason why it would be difficult for the review process to stop or slide backwards now. The public outcry over military sex scandals is about a more profound disconnect: between a significant institution which is seen to reflect a nation's identity and values, and the nature of those very ideals. If the Australian military becomes less and less representative of the community it serves and their values, that's a dangerous and unsustainable place to be, as Angus Campbell pointedly remarked in his Canberra speech.

'You become an enclave and that's a terrible thing for the army. Right now we have 12 per cent women and that's not enough. I want more of the incredible talent in the other half of the population. It's easy to see why, if you look at jobs, work and family and other matters, we are underperforming.'

And when a lot of men in the army hear about action on gender they immediately personalise it and wonder what is going to happen to them, he told me. 'We can say rationally we will build this change together. But you don't necessarily get a calm and rational analysis. You can build to that but it's not an easy start point – there's an uneasy assumption that we must be talking about fundamentally changing the gender blend in the infantry. What I'm talking about is allowing anyone to serve. So far, not surprisingly, very few women have indicated an interest in service with the infantry – it's a very physically hard job – but those few who have joined are doing fine.'

The new army norms will be about men and women working in whatever roles they can do and less about traditional soldier standards. Experienced army members like Amanda Fielding know this and even though she has reservations about how the programs to support women are faring, she also knows it's time to stop lecturing women about how they have to appear to fit in. 'I've always said to women, you don't have to act like a bloke to get on in the army but we have some women who feel they have to act like a man to get ahead and that's a sign we have to do something else – we need to talk about this and not to be one of the boys.' In fact Fielding says she believes she progressed in her career because she has been herself. 'I proved that I was fit, capable and competent. I have not tried to pretend to be someone else because I could never pull that off. I believe I have succeeded in the army due to others trusting me to be me, with my own strengths and weaknesses.'

And she knows that the work of leaders in legitimising this change is crucial. Her time in Afghanistan made that obvious: 'In the headquarters some people were very supportive but at the beginning of my tour it became clear that not everyone in the headquarters valued the work of the gender adviser. At the end of each week, the Commander of Resolute Support, General John Campbell (USA) would receive an update from the Headquarters staff. At the end of these updates, he would go around the table of general officers and then around the room of staff officers and ask for questions and every time he did this, in a room of 70 senior officers and embassy officials he would say, "Amanda, any gender issues to raise?" He knew the staff were not taking the job seriously and he let it be known very early in my tenure that it was important to him. This act was very powerful and after he started doing it, I got a lot more traction and support in my work from the Headquarters. I'll never forget that and I tell that story so people understand how important leadership support is.'

Meanwhile, the impact of powerful military men speaking and acting to change the gender status quo is symbolically significant, particularly when it comes to role modelling for the business sector. The effects are being felt well beyond organisations and across society. His work and staunch articulation of the need for gender change played a part in Morrison being appointed Australian of the Year in 2016. It was not without controversy, with some veterans' groups insisting Morrison should pay more attention to their concerns than to gender – despite his consistent work and support for these groups over many years. But he is overwhelmingly optimistic about the outlook for women in the ADF and the likelihood of progress continuing. 'There is no going back now and I am absolutely certain, in the army's case, that Angus Campbell is as completely determined to push these beneficial changes through as I was. The number of women in the army continues to grow, as do the opportunities for women, and men and women of non-Anglo Saxon heritage. I don't think the government or the Australian public would tolerate any stepping back.'

Clinging to those old notions is what the army and indeed the community have done for way too long, according to Campbell. 'I think we have absolutely had in the army, as in the rest of Australia, a period for many decades, which came to an end fifteen years ago, of the mindset that women should be projecting themselves as men to progress professionally. That idea is quite anachronistic to what we are doing and what I see around the workplace today [is that] we have really increasing qualitative improvements in decision-making and in sustainability in teams. Men and women are working together and as individuals – everything is changing.'

That strong sense that women just aren't made of the right stuff for the army is slowly and painfully being challenged – by the men in charge. Only the most optimistic would predict a smooth transition or a rapid conversion. The important message Campbell would love his successor to have is you can't take your foot off the accelerator and think it will be okay. Although he was doing everything he could to get the pipeline of female recruits flowing, it hadn't started, he admitted. But along with the changes to recruitment, training and progression criteria, Campbell knows there is a strong need to change the 'band of brothers' image. As we finish talking, he asked if I have daughters (yes, three) and then if I would encourage them to join the army. Absolutely not, I responded. 'We have to deal with the absolutely-nots', he said.

That's not the way military leaders would have reacted in the recent past. There is a growing awareness from the top that this new workplace involves dismantling gender stereotypes and debunking the long list of reasons that women are commonly believed to be ill-suited or a hindrance to the work of soldiers or sailors or pilots. And to provide evidence of a workplace that welcomes rather than penalises women. It's an uncomfortable and often ugly struggle to fight for this convincing narrative, and not just in the ADF by any means, as the next chapter examines. Fans of the story that women just need fixing have been eager to support the idea women suffer from a genetic mismatch of qualities – too much emotion and too little confidence. Try telling that to some of the remarkably talented and capable women I have met, who have spent years in the ADF – sometimes on the front lines. This version of inequality simply doesn't add up, but as we'll see, it remains hugely popular and very damaging.

CHAPTER 8

Backlash and confidence tricks

'You're the greatest threat to
Australia's security – ever.'

A MALE AUDIENCE MEMBER TO ELIZABETH BRODERICK
AT THE LAUNCH OF A REVIEW INTO THE TREATMENT OF WOMEN
IN THE AUSTRALIAN DEFENCE FORCE.

AS SEX DISCRIMINATION COMMISSIONER, ELIZABETH Broderick was used
to strong resistance to her work. Even so, it's a big call to suggest
that the fair treatment of women signals the erosion of national
security. This irate gentleman, however, was not alone. Within
the military, the strongest sign of the backlash is the constant
message to serving women that they only got the job or promotion because of their gender. And that such equal opportunity

measures are, of course, hugely 'unfair', despite men making up the vast majority of recruits and candidates for promotion. But of course, equality is in the eye of the beholder and a deep sense of entitlement (particularly in male-dominated fields) is a legacy of the male breadwinner – or in the ADF, the traditional warrior – model that many still regard as the natural order.

So yes, tempers can get frayed when all this comes up for discussion. Just the mention of any measures to give women the same opportunities as men often leads to knee-jerk accusations that standards will crumble and smoothly oiled meritocracies will be corrupted (as examined in chapter 3). It's a safe bet that many of those who resist attempts to tackle the status quo strongly believe that the system works just fine, particularly if they have fared reasonably well in it. Privilege is invisible to those who have it, as US gender academic Michael Kimmel says.

Usually this backlash falls into two broad categories: firstly, the formal resistance to changes in practices or data gathering, often based on concern about eroding merit, unnecessary red tape or just a lack of need to intervene. But many strong opponents would never admit their objections publicly, and this is where the trickier passive resistance comes in, hallmarked by personalising the problem and belittling efforts to address it. Deep down, these attitudes are usually all about fear of loss – of jobs, income, bonuses, but also of status and ultimately identity.

These are the people serving in the army who just wish everything would go back to how it was thirty years ago, as the current chief of the army, Angus Campbell, has put it. Or the small but vocal cohort of blokes at Aurizon who think men are the best at driving trains. Strong informal resistance and undermining often relies on catastrophising about the earth-shattering effects that are likely to be unleashed if targets for women are introduced, or women enter male domains. Not to mention the imminent social erosion when they spend less time managing the family and looking after children.

It's not only men who energetically resist some of the interventions for change. In some environments there's enthusiastic opposition driven by women who find, after years of trying to fit in and be just like the blokes, that diversity programs highlight their gender or single them out. They may also feel these steps paint them as victims, which they firmly reject. In the ADF, the anti-affirmative action feeling can be so strong that it's common to hear the term 'being Brodericked' used as shorthand to explain why a woman has been promoted.

I think there will be more, not less, backlash to face in coming years. That's because when the cage is really being rattled for more parity, sometimes backed by powerful men, the dissension becomes stronger. And that's what is happening at the moment. It's the sound of an entrenched system straining to get back to the old ways. And it's not all from middle-aged males. At Goldman Sachs Australia, CEO Simon Rothery acknowledges that despite lots of work, progress is still difficult and slow. When the company spoke to women returning to their roles after parenting leave it uncovered some revealing factors, he said. Some of them told him they felt uncomfortable not because of their managers' expectations, but attitudes from younger colleagues, and as a result this is a group now being targeted with education programs. Backlash is there, and you don't get rid of the sceptics by having policies about behaviour, he added. 'Where I get the most cynicism is where I will be seen to be helping a woman over a man to get into a position to be considered for promotion. But it's my role to know where the talent is, and where women are not putting themselves forward, that's uneven and I'm making it fair.'

This can be difficult terrain to navigate. It's so much easier to send women off to confidence-building or public speaking workshops that don't rock the boat. Barely a week goes by without another article or a list of tips published to help women – rarely men – deal with poor confidence, apologetic speech habits and their supposed tendency to stab each other in the back. And yes, this school of thought appears to suggest that *all* women are suffering from this shopping list of preordained inadequacies, all the time. And it sells. Books and talks on women and poor confidence and assertiveness bypasses are like honey for (queen) bees.

It's far too simplistic and dangerous to suggest that individuals who are suffering from centuries of institutionalised discrimination can fix it by tweaking their behaviour. But that hasn't stopped many from trying and prospering with packaged cures. And there are three main offenders.

THE CONFIDENCE TRICK

A few months after the 2015 launch of *The Confidence Code*, a book about women and confidence by US journalists Katty Kay and Claire Shipman, I hosted a panel discussion for Women in Media in Sydney. The speakers were an impressive lot and included the then head of ABC News, Kate Torney, and newsreader Chris Bath. We talked about the many studies, quoted in the book, that reveal women tend to rate their abilities more poorly than their male peers, or don't think they are ready for a new job. But these discussions about gender and confidence, the panel said, often overlook the systemic bias in many workplaces, and the pressure women face on the domestic front.

Encouraging women to just be more assertive implies that the barriers they are facing will then simply disappear, which the panel agreed was, at best, misleading. Taking stock of what you have to offer is important, and so is understanding you can go about self-promotion in your own way rather than mimicking a male stereotype, they added. That said, the panel agreed that assertive women often get judged more harshly than assertive men. This can mean women risk getting labelled with descriptions such as 'bossy' – which is not a compliment, as Facebook executive Sheryl Sandberg noted in her campaign to ban the word. Some of Sandberg's insights, such as this, are useful, but the theme of her book *Lean In* is similar to *The Confidence Code* – if women just get their act together and lean in at the decision-making table, they will progress a lot further. Sandberg's premise was irritating, said Bath, who had seen many women 'lean in' to little effect.

It's a massive over-simplification to explain away today's detailed evidence of gender discrimination in workplaces as a function of women lacking confidence. How does confidence get defined and measured? Have men's confidence levels ever been compared to women's? Does a failure to ask for a promotion always signal poor self-esteem? And what role do workplace attitudes play in this? I interviewed consultant Barbara Robertson about this issue when I was writing an article for the *NSW Law Society Journal*. She had been running workshops on communication skills for women in law firms for many years and said the majority attending her sessions were far from unsure about their own abilities and skills. That's the part of the package they do have, she said, and there's never any question in that area. Many are finding they are ignored or their ideas are picked up by others without recognition, and they get poor feedback in performance appraisals when it comes to areas such as leadership qualities and confidence levels, she told me.

Confidence, or the lack of it, is also conveniently seen as the problem when it comes to the pay gap. But a different reading emerges when these assumptions are researched. Women who fail to negotiate aren't necessarily beset with a confidence problem, according to Hannah Riley Bowles, a Harvard lecturer who studies gender in negotiation. They might be more accurately reading the social climate and seeing it's just not a good idea. 'The answer has more to do with how women are treated when they negotiate than it has to do with their general confidence or skills at negotiation', Bowles wrote in the *Harvard Business Review*. 'Their reticence is based on an accurate read of the social environment. Women get a nervous feeling about negotiating for higher pay because they are intuiting – correctly – that self-advocating for higher pay would present a socially difficult situation for them – more so than for men.'[1]

I've been struck by how much commentary relies on this 'confidence bypass' to explain gender discrimination, even when there is clear evidence of other factors at play. Just one example from many shows how this has become a default even when serious analysis is attempted. There's been much attention paid to how few women are in the tech sector in recent years, and I began reading an article about the reasons for the problem.[2] After establishing that many factors hold women back in the sector, including opportunities for advancement, role models, mentors and work-life balance; and pointing out the majority of women surveyed in a major study also named working in a male-dominated environment as a reason for their lack of progress; and quoting the fact that two surveys found that women get offered less money than men for the same jobs and two-thirds of men get higher offers of salaries, the article still highlighted the confidence deficiency as the main problem. Not mentioned or even suggested were factors such as the impact of behaviour by male managers on women, nor was there any data to support the strong implication that women mostly don't ask for a pay rise or even complain about their treatment – or how women who do complain are treated. The vicious attacks on women who have a profile or take a stand against sexism in tech and gaming arenas, as well as in maths and science, are examples of why a perceived lack of confidence may be regularly observed. Death and rape threats are highly effective ways to silence and debilitate women.

This thinking about confidence puts the cart before the horse. If women are constantly told they have so many gender-based qualities that make them less likely to get a break, then they'd have to be very hardened indeed not to be influenced and ground down by that message. Or to modify their behaviour. Many commentators fail to acknowledge that the lack of confidence so loudly hailed as the culprit here is actually the result of the bias and discrimination woven into the attitudes and assumptions women face every day, year in and year out. Not the cause of it.

On the other side of the equation, evidence is mounting of the pitfalls of over-confidence, so horribly evident in the hubris that led to the global financial crisis. Aside from evidence that confidence levels in women depend on context and not biology, according to economics writer Jessica Irvine, there is data showing men can suffer from too much bravado and are more 'likely to undertake more acquisitions and take on more debt than female executives'. These acquisitions yield lower returns than those of their female counterparts. If our workplace goal is 'not only gender equality but more stable and highly performing companies and economies we need to also train our men to be a little less confident in their abilities'.[3]

At the very least, we should use a great deal of caution when discussing women and confidence. Context and gender expectations play a major role in the equation, and simplistic explanations about this deficit and how to 'fix' it are mostly unhelpful and counterproductive. As with mentoring for senior women, the temptation to run women-only workshops on confidence-building may tick a diversity box and even sound like a help, when it really is often a hindrance that embeds rather than confronts stereotypes. I'm confident that running negotiating and decision-making workshops for all employees would be a better option.

SPEAKING LIKE A GIRL

Many years ago, I was editing the marketing section of the *Financial Review* and interviewed an advertising executive who was visiting from the UK. After returning to the office, I realised I needed to check a couple of facts so I rang him. 'You've got an amazing voice on the phone', he said. 'You really should think about working on a sex line.' I had never really thought much about how my voice sounded until then – and certainly never considered that form of employment.

Aside from the fact his comment was breathtakingly sexist and offensive, I was reminded of it when I read yet another article exhorting women to learn how to project their voices in meetings or lower those irritatingly high-pitched tones. Women's voices – not just what they say but how they say it – are often stereotyped in ways that men's rarely are. The nagger, the whiner, even the sex line worker, reflect some of these uniformly unflattering or inappropriate ideas of the female voice and attract a mass of remedial advice. It's confusing and contradictory – and many young women feel the same, as I hear frequently on the speaking circuit.

'Every time I speak up at meetings I get pulled aside afterwards and told I'm too emotional', a decidedly matter-of-fact young woman told me at a conference in Brisbane a week or so after the celebration of International Women's Day in 2016. She was part of an audience of about 100 women in their twenties and thirties who were spending a day away from their jobs to discuss how to accelerate change for women in the workplace. And not a moment too soon, from the nature of their questions.

'How do I deal with toxic bosses?' 'How come my ideas aren't listened to?' 'Why do I hear so much conflicting advice (but the blokes around me don't) about how I should behave at work that I don't know what to do any more?' 'How come I'm seen as aggressive when I speak up and then lectured about women needing more confidence?' The contradictions and double standards they had been facing were draining and confusing. These were well-educated women holding down management-level jobs and there was not one with a 'victim mentality' among them. But they were clearly feeling enormous frustration about the barrage of dodgy unsolicited advice they regularly faced, particularly about how to be heard at the decision-making table – or more specifically, how to speak like a man to be taken seriously.

There are many parts of the 'fixing women' approach that drive me nuts, but telling women to lower their voices, drop the qualifiers from their language and stop apologising are some of the most irritating and debilitating around. There are few aspects of how we go about our daily working lives that are more fundamental than what we say and how we say it. Start telling women to constantly police their speech because it's not good enough and you start messing with their heads and their sense of self. That's not a good platform for building confidence in themselves, either. Most of us can do with some pointers on the rather complex dynamics of meetings or presentations. But when this is wrapped in gender-specific advice to remedy a female failing, and tips are based on conforming to a male norm, the upshot is to hinder and stifle, not to help.

And it's worth examining the assumptions that some of this advice about language and speaking for women are based on to start with, because there are plenty of myths that support the idea that women need to shut up, not speak up. Or if they do have to speak, to make sure they don't sound like a stereotypical woman. A professional woman told me she was once loudly advised to keep her voice down in the office by a male colleague because she sounded just like his wife. She consoled herself that at least she wasn't his wife.

It's not too hard to find evidence of vitriol and penalties – including trivialising not just how they talk but what they say – when women speak up in public domains. And that's even when their ability to communicate forcefully is clearly an essential part of their role. Hillary Clinton was described as 'shrill' on the campaign trail, and former Australian prime minister Julia Gillard was publicly excoriated for the nasal tone of her voice during her tenure, a criticism never made of her male predecessors, who were hardly exemplary orators. The absence and illegitimacy of women's voices in public is a long-held prejudice, and was brilliantly analysed and skewered by historian and Cambridge classics professor Mary Beard in a speech she made in 2014.[4] As a host of TV documentaries, she had long been the target of loud condemnation and trolling on Twitter for, amongst other sins, having long grey hair and not wearing make-up.

Her speech focused on the way women's voices have been silenced throughout history – we're talking from ancient Greek and Roman times – and continues to this day. 'This "muteness" is not just a reflection of women's general disempowerment throughout the classical world: no voting rights, limited legal and economic independence and so on. But we're dealing with a much more active and loaded exclusion of women from public speech than that – and, importantly, it's one with a much greater impact than we usually acknowledge on our own traditions, conventions and assumptions about the voice of women. What I mean is that public speaking and oratory were not merely things that ancient women didn't do: they were exclusive practices and skills that defined masculinity as a gender.'

Advising women to pretend to be men may be a quick fix, Beard says, but it doesn't get to the heart of the problem: that authority and leadership remain a masculine endeavour. Lowering our voices will simply not change the way stereotypes stymie women from speaking or being listened to in forums. And the way we use informal language also matters. In the

Defence Force, a major 2014 study found how potent language was in excluding those who were not part of the mainstream – women, indigenous people and minority racial groups.[5] In particular, that Australian speciality of 'banter', said author Elizabeth Thomson, was used to test group membership in Australian workplaces. Although it was often seen as harmless humour, banter had quite a serious effect on those who were not part of the mainstream, and was often passive-aggressive.

At Aurizon, CEO Lance Hockridge tells me that the results from a 2015 survey found some employees' attitudes still reflect a belief that women should be seen and not heard. As a result, the company launched a 'Stand Up and Speak Up' campaign, which encourages women and men to say, 'What do you mean by that?' when they hear sexist or racist comments. The idea is to both stop the informal prejudice, and also to avoid the bystander syndrome, where even those who are uncomfortable with sexist and racist behaviour feel unable to object to what they observe for fear of backlash. The campaign was an idea generated by an internal male champions group at the company, says Donna McMahon, vice-president of Human Resources, Organisational Capability at Aurizon. And using 'What do you mean by that?' has been very effective for calling out poor behaviour in a non-threatening way that helped legitimise the discomfort these comments cause instead of sweeping them under the carpet.

What and how we communicate at work is often characterised in very stereotypical terms and underpinned by long-standing assumptions about language and gender. There are a series of myths about this, according to analysis by Oxford Professor in language and communication Deborah Cameron, and they have been largely unchallenged.[6] They include the idea that communication matters more to women, that women are more verbally skilled, that men's goals are transactional and women's relational and that the genders regularly miscommunicate with one another. If men and women communicate differently, then there is a need to adjust to clear the airwaves, she adds, but points out that somehow it's always women doing the adjusting to fit male styles of talking. It's unheard of to suggest that blokes start mimicking women because even though they may be credited with more communication skills, women's style of talking and even the expressions they use continue to be seen as less effective.

Cameron demolishes most of the myths and makes a pretty good case for challenging some of the givens I hear repeated, often by women themselves. This includes, confusingly, the ideas that women don't speak up enough or talk far too much. In fact, there's no evidence that women talk more than men, Cameron says. But plenty of popular commentary presents this as a fact, including Louann Brizendine's *The Female Brain*, which claimed that women on average utter 20000 words a day compared to men's 7000.[7] It was reported around the world, but Cameron points out that it is simply not backed by any studies. Brizendine subsequently agreed that the claim was not supported by evidence and should be deleted from her book. Indeed, a range of studies reveal that there is little difference in how much men and women speak, although there are slightly more that find men take the talking honours. In fact, some studies show men even say 'like' more often, although as the mother of three daughters in their early twenties, I remain unconvinced.

If the idea that women speak more than men does not reflect reality, Cameron asks, then why is the folk belief so persistent?

'The feminist Dale Spender once suggested an explanation: she said that people overestimate how much women talk because they think that, ideally, women would not talk at all. While that may be rather sweeping, it is true that belief in female loquacity is generally combined with disapproval of it. The folk-belief that women talk more than men persists because it provides a justification for an ingrained social prejudice.'[8]

In her blog on the same topic, Cameron also takes issue with the idea that women over-apologise because they lack confidence.[9] Instead of taking this for granted, she looked at the research and found it is mixed and inconclusive. 'Some studies have found women apologizing more than men, but others have found no difference. Which findings you give more weight to is a judgment call, and researchers have different views.' Even though women probably do apologise more, Cameron believes that when you look at the studies more closely, they do not support the idea it is a symptom of 'women's socialised unassertiveness and deference'. In fact, women saying sorry may be performing a form of emotional labour which attempts to support and help others.

The myth that women and men speak so differently that they could be from different planets adds to the burden on women. By constantly drawing attention to their supposed differences, the myth helps to maintain the prejudices that are ultimately responsible for making women unequal. 'The endless policing of women's language – their voices, their intonation patterns, the words they use, their syntax – is uncomfortably similar to the way our culture polices women's bodily appearance', says Cameron.[10] Making women self-conscious about their speech has the same effect, and distracts attention from what they are saying to how they are saying it. And telling women to fix the way they speak may seem an attractive solution, but it is not likely to solve structural inequality – in fact, it looks less like empowerment and more like victim-blaming. It also looks like a mystification: not something that helps women to understand their situation, but something that stops them from seeing it clearly and working together to change it.

As Mary Beard points out, this muteness of women in public arenas has a long heritage. And it applies across the world of paid work. These days, women are also sadly missing in action when it comes to the most powerful cultural agenda setters – the movies and the news media. Analysis of movie dialogue shows women get far fewer opportunities to speak than men overall, according to data by website Polygraph, which examined the speaking parts of actors in 2000 films. 'Women between 22 and 31 delivered 37 per cent of the dialogue, but by the time they were in their 30s, that dropped to 31 per cent. Women aged between 42 and 65 had just 20 per cent of the lines and over 65s delivered three per cent of dialogue in the films studied. Women delivered the majority of dialogue (between 60 and 90 per cent) in just 166 films, whereas men were dominant in 1195 films. So-called gender parity was reached in 324 films.'[11] And women are also poorly represented behind the camera: launching a $5 million program, Gender Matters, to address this in 2015, Screen Australia revealed data showing the imbalance is most notable in traditional film, with women accounting for 32 per cent of producers, 23 per cent of writers and only 16 per cent of directors.[12]

In my own domain of the media, the lack of women quoted in or writing articles and appearing as expert commentators on

TV and radio has at last begun to attract some overdue attention around the world.[13] Women's Leadership Institute Australia found that female sources accounted for 20 per cent of all news commentary in Australia's major metro and national newspapers; in New Zealand's 2014 election coverage, 71 per cent of sources used were male.[14] Analysis in 2013 by *New Matilda* also found men dominated the senior ranks of media in Australia, while women wrote a third of opinion pieces and articles in 27 publications.[15] When it came to business coverage, the people quoted in stories in these mastheads were more than 90 per cent male, while men dominated politics, business and international news commentary. There are similar studies from the US and the UK where, despite entering the media in higher numbers than men, women are failing to be heard or interviewed at anywhere near the same rate.

Business meetings are another arena where women are often castigated for how they are speaking or not speaking. This is usually attributed to lack of confidence (see above), although being interrupted and talked over is a powerful deterrent that seems to be left out of the deficit explanation. It's women's fault again – either we speak too much and nag or don't say enough. As Cameron points out, women don't stay quiet in meetings because they are all scared or lack confidence – they do it because they want to counter the perception they are interlopers and not draw attention or criticism. These are actually problem solving strategies, she says, and to do not with how women are but the position they are put in. 'The problem is not that men and women have different communication styles, but that whatever style women use they are liable to be judged by different standards', she says. The likelihood of being interrupted while speaking in a meeting is far higher if you are a woman.

Actually, the boring droning voices you most often hear in a business meeting are likely to be male – a syndrome so aptly described by Australian writer Julia Baird as the 'manologue'.[16] 'The prevalence of the manologue is deeply rooted in the fact that men take, and are allocated, more time to talk in almost every professional setting. Women self-censor, edit, apologize for speaking. Men expound. Of course, some women can be equally long-winded, but it is far less common. The fact that this tendency is masculine has been well established in social science. The larger the group, the more likely men are to speak (unless it is in a social setting like a lunch break). One study, conducted by researchers at Brigham Young University and Princeton, found that when women are outnumbered, they speak for between a quarter and a third less time than the men.'

Some companies have introduced 'no interruptions' rules at meetings. And Sheryl Sandberg suggests taking a leaf out of President Obama's book: 'When President Obama held his last news conference of 2014, he called on eight reporters – all women. It made headlines worldwide'.[17] Sometimes other meeting protocols ensure everyone is routinely given a chance to speak up. I've seen that in action at the Defence Force advisory board meetings, where the Chief of the Defence Force, Mark Binskin, always asks everyone around the table for input.

Around the world, a range of men have also publicly committed to boycotting conferences that fail to include reasonable numbers of female speakers and panellists. It's an idea Stephen Fitzgerald, one of the first Male Champions of Change and former CEO of Goldman Sachs Australia, happily admits the group pinched and turned into the Panel Pledge, in an effort to eradicate the male-only panel, or the 'manel' as it's known. Others who are leading by example include Hans Schulz, vice-president for the Inter-American Development Bank.[18] Having attended 22 conferences in 2015 and then calculated the number of speakers and their gender, he found just 20 per cent were women. His response was to set up a database of qualified women who are 'conference ready'. His work is part of a range of moves to address the problem; Owen Barder at the London School of Economics has been recruiting men to sign a pledge: 'At a public conference I won't serve on a panel of two people or more unless there is at least one woman on the panel, not including the Chair.'

In 2016, Australian behavioural scientist and a regular on the conference circuit, Darren Hill, joined with other male public speakers to also declare they would no longer appear on manels.[19] He noted the 'irony that five white males are taking a stand against all-male panels – it's not lost on us. But fortunately we can have some influence, so we're using it.' The failure to find women as speakers is lazy and, at worst, deeply misogynistic, he pointed out. The fact that in April 2016, US company PayPal convened an all-male panel to discuss gender equality and inclusion in the workplace – of all things – was 'surely a pulse check of a deeply ingrained brogrammer culture'. Suggested steps to help avoid the 'manel' include choosing women first, then inviting the rest of the panel; asking male speakers for recommendations of female candidates; and thinking beyond the norm when putting together a panel list so that there is diversity in the line-up. (This group has also set up a register for those who want to join: www.speakerdiversity.com.)

Interestingly, Hill also described how going public with the declaration attracted plenty of sniping, dire warnings and even suggestions that such a tactic meant that all-female TV panel shows such as *The View* should be canned. That might be a relief to many (I can safely declare I have never watched it) but this is an all-too-familiar and distracting response when there is direct action to address gender imbalances. It's a false comparison to contrast the panel for a TV chat show with, say, the experts presenting on international economic trends at Davos. And it also ignores something quite fundamental that male advocates have cottoned on to: a panel pledge is not about tokenism or putting more women than men on stage. It is needed to make sure a range of the best contributors are included, rather than letting sexism narrow the options. It then allows women and their concerns to be legitimised and part of mainstream commentating, where men have long dominated.

Doing nothing has delivered nothing when it comes to who gets the stage or the microphone, and the idea that there are not enough qualified women to step up to the podium doesn't stack up these days. Efforts like the panel pledge tick a whole of boxes: they are public, they are simple to implement and they are starting to make organisers think again about who they select. And powerful men are key to making them work.

WOMEN ARE THEIR OWN WORST ENEMIES

And here we arrive at a quintessential and particularly contradictory manifestation of the gender deficit model. Not only are women shooting themselves in the foot simply by being women, they are also predisposed to shoot (or stab) other women, especially if they are successful, because they turn into 'queen bees'.

Where to begin with this beehive of silliness and sexism? If I've heard this once I've heard it just about every time I speak about gender, and given the theme of this book and the strength of the backlash, it is getting even louder.

The 'uber-bitch in the office' is a magnetic figure and reinforces all those latent suspicions that women are not built for competitive workplaces, which naturally bring out the worst in them (but not in men, apparently). Thus this classic mismatch inflames innate female nastiness and back-stabbing. The glee in perpetuating this line of thinking is rarely dampened by asking how this compares to male behaviour and norms. Or whether this lack of scrutiny means we are disproportionately focusing once again on how women behave or misbehave because of stereotypical expectations. Woe betide women who fail to be nice or who disagree with each other.

So here are a few myth busters: there's no hard evidence that a majority of women behave like queen bees once they access power, in fact the research on which this assumption rests consists of just one study, conducted in 1974 (by researchers GL Staines, TE Jayaratne, and C Tavris).[20] It suggested that women who are successful in male-dominated environments were more likely to endorse gender stereotypes, and view other women as competitors. But once again, while this can happen, it's crucial to examine why it happens, and how often. Other research has also suggested that the rare cohort of women who do finally crash through the glass ceiling can be more inclined to reflect back the norms of the power group they have joined. And that can mean exhibiting bias against women aspiring to senior jobs. (And at the risk of repeating myself, shouldn't that also mean the norms have to change, not the women? Just saying.)

I haven't been a fan of framing solutions to gender problems as a simple case of 'leaning in'. It's just way too simplistic and ignores too many of the ways bias operates in your average workspace. So I did feel a sense of relief to read an article by Sheryl Sandberg in mid-2016 as I was finishing this book which argued against the idea of the queen bee and bitchy women syndrome.[21] In fact women aren't any nastier to each other than other human beings – they are just expected to be nicer, she concluded. Alleluia.

These findings shouldn't be seen as support for categorising women as better behaved than men, either. Of course women sometimes behave badly to each other. We are human beings and goodness comes no more easily or naturally to us than to anyone else. I know I am hardly perfect but then again the men I know and work with aren't either. And clearly no-one should engage in destructive behaviour in the workplace. Full stop. So why do women so often become the target of this accusation? Many studies and observations suggest there are particular circumstances that may contribute: being shut out of power and having to fight extra hard to get ahead and then being scrutinised much more than the blokes around you for example. I've certainly seen instances of the 'not me' syndrome where senior women go out of their way to deny they have suffered gender discrimination, and are tougher on women to prove it, rather than supportive. I worked for a woman who was the least sympathetic of all my senior colleagues to the agenda on women's rights (and also worked with many more women who were the opposite). But her trenchant views always seemed to me a reaction to and irritation with the double standards she had faced. And who knows what the ratio of 'queen bees' is to other women – even in 1973 when the original study was done, but particularly now?

Perhaps unsurprisingly, some strong research since that original study has shown that the exact opposite can also be revealed in organisations. According to a 2012 Catalyst report, 'many of the men and women currently involved in talent development had themselves been developed by someone else. Of this group, 65 per cent of women who had received career support went on to return the favor to the next batch of emerging leaders, compared to 56 per cent of men in the same situation. Out of the women who said they were developing talent, 73 per cent said they are developing other women. This contradicts the idea that the majority of powerful women are Queen Bees who discriminate against the women they supervise.'[22]

Likewise, more recent evidence doesn't show that women consistently and routinely fail to support or benefit from having other women around them. In fact, women are more positive about leadership when they see more women in these roles, according to a 2015 report.[23] In brief, the study of 600 leaders found that especially in male-dominated organisations, when female leaders don't see many other examples of people like them, they felt under pressure to conform to male-associated leadership qualities and expected behaviours. But 'women in organizations with proportionally more women held a more positive gender identity and experienced less identity conflict'. Working in organisations where being a woman, with the associated strengths, is seen as explicitly positive left women more motivated to lead.[24]

The bitchy stereotype is part of our recurring focus on the penalties incurred by women in the workplace. It has enthusiastic supporters – male and female – and is trotted out with alarming regularity. The problem is that the more we reinforce a stereotype the more we embed the problem, rather than challenging it. We expect women to have unquestioned loyalty to their gender, no matter what that may impose or how much penalising it incurs. Sharon Mavin, a UK academic, has found that assumptions senior women will behave with solidarity to their gender cannot be fulfilled and are not applied to men.[25] Continued use of the 'queen bee' label, without acknowledgement of the embedded gendered context for women in senior management, perpetuates a 'blame the woman' perspective and a 'one-woman responsibility', her research suggests. While male misbehaviour in the workplace does of course get scrutinised, and male stereotypes are relied on to explain transgressions such as sexual harassment, other examples of poor form are rarely attributed to gender-wide failings. Men rarely get told their gender is to blame for failing to support each other on the job, or not putting others ahead of themselves, nor are they told there is a special place in hell for men who don't help other men.

These double standards are reinforced by a constant focus on female faults – women's confidence, their speech, their insecurity and interaction with each other – which is ridiculously generic and stereotype-driven. And it tells us a lot about the behaviour and characteristics we are still telling ourselves are most valued in Australian workplaces. Research consistently finds that 'the way we do things around here' serves white men better than women and people of colour, says gender consultant Deborah May. No, not all white men, but those who somehow 'fit' the unconscious notion of who we expect to see in particular roles, disciplines, industries and functions. And in Australia, what we value is shaped by outdated notions of cultural fit that includes the happy-go-lucky good-looking bloke with a bit of jaunty bravado, good sportsmanship, mateship and loyalty. They may be outdated but these norms, according to May, still have an impact on decisions and assessments about the type of person 'suitable' for particular roles – especially in the most senior positions.

Simply being a woman in the workforce over the past few decades has meant facing multiple messages about a litany of gender-specific faults that only women can address. It is all based on the same fabricated story about traditional female weakness, and unsuitability for leadership, and it offers dodgy advice as a solution to deeply embedded structural biases. It is also usually banal and downright contradictory: women are either too bolshy, too timid, too loud, too quiet, too friendly, too isolated, too risk averse, too soft, too nasty, or too lacking in ambition. And so it goes on. The deficit model has a lot to answer for. What becomes crystal clear is that no amount of lecturing women and ignoring the systemic advantages given to the male breadwinner will change the dynamics of power and those who wield it.

When leaders and men in particular challenge this story and intervene, the tables can turn. But no-one in power goes down without a fight. Backlash means you are doing something right, according to former army chief David Morrison. I asked him how he tackled it. 'By repeating the positive messages over and over and over. By taking heart that when there is hostile and vitriolic criticism you must be doing something right. By staring down the naysayers and using the plethora of evidence to point out that diversity improves the corporate bottom line. By keeping the faith, confident that you are making a difference.'

CONCLUSION

And where to from here?

'Once you've seen gender
discrimination you can't unsee it.'

DAVID MORRISON

IN 2011 A GROUP OF researchers looking at many years of data
about US car accidents discovered that women were 47 per cent
more likely to be seriously injured than men. Although previous studies had looked at differences in men's and women's
driving to explain the discrepancy, the researchers suggested
the safety features in cars, such as head support and airbags,
were mostly designed for average male dimensions and could be
leaving women more susceptible to injuries. Even the car crash

dummies used in testing were based on a standard male body, they found.[1]

I first came across this example in a report put together by Australian Women Donors Network, a philanthropic body that advises on why and how to direct funding to programs that benefit women and girls.[2] Just like the car crash investigators, AWDN found that if philanthropic donations are not viewed through a 'gender lens', women in need can miss out on critical support. That ability to see the world through a different set of eyes also helped transform David Morrison into a vocal campaigner for women's rights, a mantle he continues to proudly wear well after leaving the army.

Once you see the impact of refocusing from fixing women to getting serious backing for fixing the bias and recalibrating the power equation in workplaces, you can't unsee that either. As this analysis has shown, the remedial model is tenacious and pervasive, possibly even stronger because of the increased attention and the use of levers such as targets to address gender imbalances these days. Researchers are seeing the same trend – Melbourne Business School professor of organisational management Isabel Metz, agreed that not only is victim blaming still around, but it is being encouraged and reinforced.

Until recently many organisations and the people who run them have suffered from an acute lack of motivation and a fair bit of wilful blindness when confronted with the need to build a fairer workplace. Siphoning women into confidence-building seminars doesn't rock the boat or involve uncomfortable and confronting discussions about fairness and power. It also hasn't made much difference to gender imbalances. But as we've seen, it does make a difference to dismantle rigid working regimes and recognise caring demands; ensure the work of women and minority groups is appropriately assessed and rewarded; challenge the bias woven through those beliefs about 'merit' and progression; or to audit pay.

Of course many of the organisations examined here are just beginning to make these changes. As more employers recognise the benefit from stopping ineffective remedial measures, they will also start to see the upside of addressing structural bias so all employees can fully contribute and boost results. The traditional ways of work aren't just old-fashioned – they are failing to deliver for men, women and employers. The interventions described here are stepping stones to fairer conditions, not a short cut to overtake men or get a free ride. Indeed, when these steps achieve better outcomes they become redundant. In the meantime, circuit breakers are needed because, as Lance Hockridge and Martin Parkinson both point out, if nothing is done to disrupt the status quo then we will go on getting the same gender outcomes and poor economic returns we always have.

These often unpopular and confronting moves to recalibrate the workplace are not about letting men once again take the limelight, but about men learning to give some of it up. It's about ensuring the people in the corner office clearly see this agenda as a legitimate organisational improvement not just for women, but ultimately for all employees. There are many men who are taking this agenda seriously, either through groups such as the Male Champions of Change, or under their own steam. And while many now understand the problem and its implications, they also appreciate that there are no simple answers.

Ahmed Fahour, CEO at Australia Post and one of the few Australian business leaders who is not from an Anglo-Saxon background, bluntly told an audience in late 2016, 'If we can't get something as plainly obvious as gender equality right then what hope does anybody else have who is slightly different? What does it mean for minorities? What does it mean for indigenous people? And it's depressing if you are at that end of the room, and we can't as a society get gender equality right. So I kind of get pretty despondent about this.'[3]

I have my moments of despondency too; it's an occupational hazard. But a shift which is legitimising this as a key business problem has accelerated in the last few years: even the fact that Fahour is making these comments at a business forum reflects this refocusing. Of course there must be more than words and some tangible results across the areas examined here – including more examples of men ensuring women are put in roles where they can influence outcomes. It is only when women occupy positions of substantial power and influence, in more than trivial numbers, that they are able to shape a company's overall stance toward gender equity in a way that results in meaningful progress, as US academic William Bielby has pointed out.[4]

I've seen that dynamic at close quarters. I spent a few months in 2015 working with the initiative established by former ANZ executive Joyce Phillips, who ran a campaign called Equal Future to encourage more women to become financially literate – a goal that clearly dovetailed with her role as head of global wealth for the bank. But she did far more than just her job. She not only helped lobby for superannuation top-ups for female employees (described in chapter 4) with low retirement savings balances, but started a website and provided free financial advice for women. She asked me to write a series of columns about sexism in practice – the stuff that can be hard to detect and address – which was titled 'Enough'. Her frustration with the lack of progress was palpable and her response was practical. Her leadership was crucial.

Only those with clout – men and women – can confront the rules. Instead of reminding groups of women they aren't good enough, progress will come from changing what Bielby calls management regimes: the practices, routines, understandings and values that define how organisations approach their commitments and obligations to diversity. That's why some of the employers examined here stand a much better chance of making headway: they aim to match reality with the rhetoric. And many recognise that what creates and sustains gender bias in the workplace is not all in our heads, as Bielby pointed out, nor is it 'mostly about the cognitive errors of well-intentioned managers and supervisors who want to do the right thing if only we would give them the training that tells them what that might be. It is fundamentally about how we structure organisations and how we structure work […] and about the degree to which the everyday practice of hiring, assigning, developing, training, and promoting men and women is tightly or loosely coupled with what companies claim are their policies and practices regarding anti-discrimination and diversity.'

That is a job for everyone, not just for women. Inequality is not and has never been a women's problem, Deborah Gillis, the CEO of US women and work research firm Catalyst explained when I asked for her thoughts on this proposition. 'Our biggest failure as a society is that we haven't held everyone accountable for the barriers that continue to be placed upon women in the workplace. Women are not being held back simply because of "unconscious biases" or "hidden biases" or other factors beyond our control. They are experiencing many obstacles – at work and in the world – which are the result of fear of change, comfort with the status quo, a lack of awareness of the role privilege plays, and exclusion from others.' Engagement with men as allies can change workplaces, she added, and change lives.

Beyond the workplace, there are some welcome signs that automatically blaming the victim for gender discrimination and violence against women is being challenged. The work of domestic violence campaigners, such as 2015 Australian of the Year Rosie Batty, and the steps being taken by the ADF have helped build momentum. Awareness is growing of the need to address the causes by examining the strong link between gender inequality and violence against women, and a focus on perpetrators. This has not been an overnight switch but it's a reframing that was unimaginable just a few years ago when it was common to hear that women wearing high heels and short skirts were asking for trouble. Now the level of awareness has been transformed and there has even been business action as well as talk: Telstra is one of several large employers to introduce domestic violence leave in recent years, with several reporting employees have made use of this important provision.

Something fundamental has to shift in the gender and workplace debate too: the deeply imbued story of women as poorly equipped interlopers in the realm of paid work who need a makeover. Women have in fact always worked to sustain themselves and their families, as any social historian can tell you, but this narrative continues to resonate in the rigid ways organisational leadership is defined, jobs are structured and rewarded, and expectations reinforced about who will do the domestic work. The strong adherence to the male ideals of the Aussie digger and the Anzac legend in the ADF, and the male breadwinner norm, are reminders of why recalibrating the story is clearly no simple task. You need very clear vision, analysis and tenacity to interrogate and change these beliefs.

You also need the top executives with clout, and many quoted here are making that investment. They realise you can't just say you believe in better gender outcomes, you have to be personally accountable. Men who really want to see gender equality become a reality need to not just step up, but occasionally step aside too, as Australian feminist Clementine Ford has pointed out.[5] It's no good just calling yourself a feminist, which has become quite the thing to do among white, middle-aged, powerful men: you have to also show you mean it. Like the Canadian politician Ted McMeekin, who stepped down as a minister of municipal affairs in Ontario in 2016 so he could help achieve 'gender parity' in the cabinet. Now that's a feminist. It will be a sign of real progress when male feminists are unremarkable and women, particularly those in power, feel free to describe themselves as feminists without being pilloried.

Meanwhile, however, the fight to stop blaming women and build a fairer workplace is about much more than political correctness or hurt feelings from missing out on a promotion. Many women at all levels throughout the workforce face the impact of discrimination and stereotyping as they confront sexism and bias in offices and factories, from one incident to the next. The impact is serious: it's about being the last to get shifts or pay rises or first for redundancy. And those who speak out often pay a high price. It's easy to forget that just a few years ago, the CEO of Australian retailer David Jones, Mark McInnes, resigned after two formal complaints of harassment from a young female employee, who had followed the HR protocol to the letter. The 2010 incident provoked rampant victim-blaming as the young woman was widely pilloried, and she eventually left Australia. McInnes, meanwhile, was soon appointed to another executive role.

Six years later, however, the on-air 'joke' that media personality and AFL club president Eddie McGuire made about a well-known female sports journalist being drowned did attract a different reaction. His tasteless comments were criticised – not the woman he attacked – by plenty of men too. That reaction was a sign, Martin Parkinson, told me, of real change around these issues that simply wouldn't have occurred even a few years ago. David Morrison agrees there is a shift occurring. 'Call me naive, but I think we are at something of a tipping point and having men's voices being heard as agents of change is having an impact.'

These are encouraging signs but I asked if he thought the penny was dropping about changing focus from women to the workplace. 'I do, but we have hardly arrived in Camelot yet. I think that the current focus on the real benefits of diversity – creative thinking and giving opportunities for more people to reach their potential – is very much the correct approach. As I increasingly engage with the corporate and public sector world I sense that there is a change in thinking underway, but progress, as measured by the number of women at more senior levels, and on boards, is haphazard and in some respects glacial. Nonetheless, the message is well and truly out there that this is not about "fixing" women but rather growing more capable workforces.'

There are many reminders of the challenges in amplifying that message. I finished off my writing against the backdrop of a brutal and toxic US presidential campaign, where gender and power took centre stage, and the defeat of the highly qualified Hillary Clinton by a man who had boasted of sexual assault left many in a state of shock. Although some analysts claimed gender was not a factor in the election of Donald Trump, it is hard to believe that the demonisation of Clinton, which had been building over decades, would have had the same resonance if a man with similar strengths and failings had been the Democractic nominee. The sexism and double standards faced by Clinton reminded many Australians of the treatment of prime minister Julia Gillard. These appalling examples show a substantial social shift is needed to change norms around the treatment of women at all levels in the workplace and society.

The outcry over Trump's comments about women shouldn't be dismissed as a sideshow or trivial. It's essential to keep the objections to sexism up because it can make a difference to the big picture on gender bias too, as academic neuropsychologist Cordelia Fine explained.[6] Masculinity and femininity were once thought of as polar ends of a span, but more and more brain research has revealed the basic differences between the sexes are small or modest in size at most. Knowing someone is male or female doesn't predict their behaviour, she said, but decades of research has shown essentialist thinking – that we are born essentially female or male to our back teeth – deepens social divides. And essentialism has given scientific legitimacy to gender stereotypes that keeps the sexes in different spheres with unequal status. Gender constructivism, on the other hand, sees people's environment as part of the equation but in a way that interacts with biology.

This construction of gender is like sewing a tapestry, according to Fine, with many threads involved in making up the picture. So picking at the threads to unravel the stereotypes is important, and that's why calling out small acts of sexism is crucial. People who speak up don't deserve to be shot down as 'politically correct' or whinging or trivial. After all, she said, when there is no single influence that contributes to our picture of gender and every influence is modest, if no-one sweats the small stuff, how will the big picture of the gender tapestry ever change?

Sweating the small stuff and changing the big picture means leaving the deficit story about women in the workplace where it belongs: in the past. To do that we need a new framing of the business and economic case for improving gender fairness. With this in mind, I read about the demographic shift that has seen a significant increase in the number of single women in the West over the last few decades. As journalist Gaby Hinsliff pointed out, the thesis of Rebecca Traister's book *All the Single Ladies* is that this group don't want to be told to get a husband but they do have different expectations. 'They'd rather the economy was reshaped around women's changing lives than vice versa', Hinsliff wrote.[7]

That's what I'd concluded too. Employers and their leaders holding on to traditional gender norms of primary male earners and women as secondary income providers need to adapt to the realities of their workforces and future markets for their goods and services rather than the other way around. But no great shift in the status of women as citizens and workers (and increasingly breadwinners), nor any civil or human rights movement, can succeed purely through the efforts of the marginalised group. Just about every ultimate victory in fighting slavery and racism, and winning basic voting rights for women, had to be eventually supported and championed by established male power groups which, usually reluctantly, had to give up some of their entitlement to help tackle injustice. As the male leaders quoted here reveal, powerful men like them *are* the system so they need to do more than stop fixing women or joining them on the barricades – they need to fix themselves.

Sometimes resonant and timely messages come from unlikely places. I was reading Oxford professor of language Deborah Cameron's book *The Myth of Mars and Venus*, and she mentioned receiving a postcard which seemed to sum up the frustration of dealing with stubborn and destructive gender stereotyping.[8] Not long after, I found the same card in my favourite London bookshop. It is sitting in front of me now: 'Men are from earth. Women are from earth. Deal with it.' Amen to that.

Acknowledgments

My thanks to all those women who provide inspiration and often coffee: including Aviva Lowy, Judith Hoare, Geraldine Fox, Rosemary Johnston, Beverley Uther, Helen Trinca, Margot Saville, Jane Caro, Michele Jackson, Carmel McGregor, Julie McKay, Adele Miles, Janet Morrison, Heather McIlwain, Annika Freyer, Jane Counsel, Miriam Silva, Rae Cooper, Diane Smith-Gander, Kathryn Fagg, Wendy McCarthy, Anne Summers, Ann Sherry, Cassandra Kelly, Kirsten Galliott, Narelle Hooper, Fiona Smith, Beverley Head, Helen Connealy, Tracey Spicer, Marina Go, Sally Patten, Karen Maley, Susan Ferrier, Elizabeth Broderick, Alex Shehadie, Deanne Weir, Julie Reilly, Carol Schwartz, Joyce Phillips, Julia Baird, Ros Kelly, Annabel Crabb, Yolanda Beattie, Eve Mahlab, Claire Braund and Ruth Medd.

And thanks also to those who gave up time to talk or be interviewed: Elizabeth Proust, David Morrison, Angus Campbell, Jennifer Whelan, Neil Cockcroft, James Sutherland, Amanda Fielding, Deborah May, Simon Rothery, Lance Hockridge, Martin Parkinson, Stephen Fitzgerald, Deborah Gillis, Graeme Russell, Andrew Stevens and Robert Wood.

As always the support from the team at NewSouth Publishing, particularly Phillipa McGuinness, is much appreciated. And where would I be without my daughters Simone, Evie and Antonia?

Notes

Introduction

1   Fiona Smith, 'Privilege is invisible to those who have it: engaging men in workplace gender equality', *The Guardian*, 8 June 2016, <www.theguardian.com/sustainable-business/2016/jun/08/workplace-gender-equality-invisible-privilege>, accessed 23 December 2016.

2   World Economic Forum, 'The case for gender equality', *The global gender gap report 2015*, 19 November 2015, <reports.weforum.org/global-gender-gap-report-2015/the-case-for-gender-equality/?doing_wp_cron=1475850 086.8222110271453857421875>, accessed 23 December 2016.

3   John Daley, 'Game-changers: Economic reform priorities for Australia', Grattan Institute, June 2012, p. 39, <grattan.edu.au/wp-content/uploads/2014/04/Game_Changers_Web.pdf>, accessed 23 December 2016.

4   Ross Clare, 'Developments in the level and distribution of retirement savings', Association of Superannuation Funds of Australia, September 2011, p. 2, <1403-LevelAndDistributionRetirementSavings-2.pdf>, accessed 23 December 2016.

5   NSW Department of Industry, 'Key statistics about women entrepreneurs in Australia', NSW Department of Industry, February 2016, <www.industry.nsw.gov.au/__data/assets/pdf_file/0005/81968/fact-sheet-women-in-business.pdf>, accessed 23 December 2016.

6   Jenny Anderson, 'This is progress? The newest CEOs are less worldly and more male than ever', *Quartz*, 19 April 2016, <qz.com/664888/this-is-progress-the-newest-ceos-are-less-worldly-and-more-male-than-ever/>, accessed 23 December 2016.

7   McKinsey, 'Women in the workplace 2016', McKinsey&Company, September 2016, <www.mckinsey.com/business-functions/organization/our-insights/women-in-the-workplace-2016?cid=other-eml-nsl-mip-mck-oth-1610>, accessed 23 December 2016.

8   Kimberlé Williams Crenshaw, 'Mapping the margins: Intersectionality, identity politics and violence against women of color', *Stanford Law Review*, vol 43, July 1991, p. 1242, <www.mckinsey.com/business-functions/organization/our-insights/women-in-the-workplace-2016?cid=other-eml-nsl-mip-mck-oth-1610>, accessed 23 December 2016.

1 From victim blaming to system shaming

1   Male Champions of Change, 'Accelerating the advancement of women', Human Rights Commission, 2013, <www.humanrights.gov.au/sites/default/files/document/publication/2013_AHRC_MCC_accelerating_advancement_women.pdf>, accessed 23 December 2016.

2   Primrose Riordan, 'Martin Parkinson's gender changes to be public service model', *Australian Financial Review*, 31 January 2016, <www.afr.com/news/martin-parkinsons-gender-changes-to-be-public-service-model-20160130-gmhram#ixzz45uN0cn43>, accessed 23 December 2016.

3   Isabel Metz, 'Male champions of gender equity change', Melbourne Business School, June 2016, <mbs.edu/getmedia/48007aa7-4bae-454d-91a9-e1fb4df7b8dc/Male-Champions-of-Gender-Equity-Change-Report-double-page.pdf>, accessed 23 December 2016.

4   Naomi Woodley, 'Gender neutral travel policies a must for sports bodies wanting funding, Government says', *ABC News Online*, 3 February 2016, <www.abc.net.au/news/2016-02-03/gender-neutral-travel-policies-a-must-for-sports-bodies-ley/7134966>, accessed 23 December 2016.

5   ABC News, 'Fact check: did the 2015–16 Women's Big Bash League attract more viewers than the men's A League?', *ABC News Online*, 3 April 2016, <www.abc.net.au/news/2016-04-03/fact-check-does-womens-big-bash-league-outrate-the-a-league/7253846>, accessed 23 December 2016.

6   Peter Lalor, 'Australia's female cricketers win big pay rise but still earn far less than men', *The Australian*, 6 April 2016, <www.theaustralian.com.au/sport/cricket/australias-female-cricketers-win-big-pay-rise-but-still-earn-far-less-than-men/news-story/01e20bee44815af9816e6fec9e349929>, accessed 23 December 2016.

7   Adam Galinsky and Maurice Schweitzer, 'It's good to be the Queen...but it's easier being the King', McKinsey&Company, September 2015, <www.mckinsey.com/global-themes/leadership/its-good-to-be-the-queen-but-its-easier-being-the-king>, accessed 23 December 2016.

8   Catherine Fox and Heather McIlwain, 'The Treasury', *CEW Case Studies*, 2014, <cew.org.au/wp-content/uploads/2016/07/CEW_CaseStudy_TheTreasury1.pdf>, accessed 23 December 2016.

9   Melanie Sanders, Jayne Hrdlicka, Meredith Hellicar, Dale Cottrell and Joanna Knox,, 'What stops women from reaching the top?', CEW/Bain&Company, November 2011, <www.bain.com/offices/australia/en_us/Images/BAIN_BRIEF_What_stops_women_from_reaching_the_top.pdf>, accessed 23 December 2016.

10 AWCCI Media Release, 'National Research findings: Women are shaping the new economy', March 2012, <www.awcci.org.au/news/media-releases/12-media-release/70-national-research-findings-women-are-shaping-the-new-economy.html>, accessed 23 December 2016.

11 AWCCI, 'The Issues Paper: Collection of sex desegregated data and the procurement of contracts for women business owners in Australia', August 2012, <www.awcci.org.au/speak-up/recommendations.html>, accessed 23 December 2016.

12 Bruce Billson, 'Women trailblazing small business in Australia', Treasury Portfolio Ministers media release, 7 March 2015, <bfb.ministers.treasury.gov.au/media-release/020-2015/>, accessed 23 December 2016.

13 Australian Bureau of Statistics, 'Profile of Australian women in business', Office of Women, 2015, <www.dpmc.gov.au/sites/default/files/publications/profile_of_australian_women_in_business_0.pdf>, accessed 23 December 2016.

14 Denholm Sadler, 'Startup Muster 2015 report shows Australia is "on the precipice of something amazing"', startupsmart, 4 December 2015, <www.startupsmart.com.au/advice/growth/startup-muster-2015-report-shows-australia-is-on-the-precipice-of-something-amazing/>, accessed 23 December 2016.

15 Knowledge@Wharton, 'Why VCs Aren't Funding Women-led Startups', Knowledge@Wharton, 24 May 2016, <knowledge.wharton.upenn.edu/article/vcs-arent-funding-women-led-startups/>, accessed 23 December 2016.

16 Meraiah Foley, 'Becoming a "mumpreneur" is an option of last resort for many working mothers', *The Sydney Morning Herald*, 4 May 2016, <www.smh.com.au/comment/becoming-a-mumpreneur-is-an-option-of-last-resort-for-many-working-mothers-20160504-golrkl.html#ixzz483kjaNvI>, accessed 23 December 2016.

2 The fight for flexibility

1   Melanie Sanders, Jennifer Zeng, Meredith Hellicar and Kathryn Fagg, 'The Power of Flexibility: A Key Enabler to Boost Gender Parity and Employee Engagement', *Bain&Company Insights*, 4 February 2016, <www.bain.com/publications/articles/the-power-of-flexibility.aspx>, accessed 23 December 2016.

2   Australian Bureau of Statistics, 'Profile of Australian women in business', Office of Women, 2015, <www.dpmc.gov.au/sites/default/files/publications/profile_of_australian_women_in_business_0.pdf>, accessed 23 December 2016.

3 Sanders, Zeng, Hellicar and Fagg, 2016.

4 Sanders, Zeng, Hellicar and Fagg, 2016.

5 Luke Graham, 'Why men (at least pretend to) work longer hours', NBC News, 4 June 2015, <www.nbcnews.com/business/careers/why-men-least-pretend-work-longer-hours-n369731?cid=sm_fb>, accessed 23 December 2016.

6 Greg Jericho, 'Australian men are leaners not lifters in the housework department', *The Guardian*, 4 June 2014.

7 Moira Weigel, 'The foul reign of the biological clock', *The Guardian*, 10 May 2016.

8 Weigel, 2016.

9 Australian Human Rights Commission, 'Supporting working parents: Pregnancy and Return to Work National Review Report', Australian Human Rights Commission, October 2014, <www.humanrights.gov.au/publications/supporting-working-parents-pregnancy-and-return-work-national-review-report/chapter-2>, accessed 23 December 2016.

10 Radhika Sanghani, 'Three-quarters of mothers experience discrimination at work', *The Telegraph*, 22 March 2016, <www.telegraph.co.uk/women/work/three-quarters-of-mothers-experience-discrimination-at-work/>, accessed 23 December 2016.

11 Sanders, Zeng, Hellicar and Fagg, 2016.

12 Susie Babani, 'Don't fight flexible work. It's productive. And it's already here.' *ANZ BlueNotes*, 19 August 2015, <bluenotes.anz.com/posts/2015/08/dont-fight-flexible-work/>, accessed 23 December 2016.

13 Misa Han, 'Caltex bonus convinces all mums to return to work', *Australian Financial Review*, 5 November 2015, <www.afr.com/news/caltex-bonus-convinces-all-mums-to-return-to-work-20151103-gkpuyp>, accessed 23 December 2016.

14 Jane Gilmore, 'Flexible working in the Australian Defence Force', *Women's Agenda*, 25 November 2015, <www.womensagenda.com.au/talking-about/editors-agenda/item/6553-flexible-working-arrangements-in-the-australian-defence-force>, accessed 23 December 2016.

15 Lynda Gratton and Andrew Scott, *The 100-year life*, Bloomsbury, London, 2016.

16 Gratton and Scott 2016, p. 189.

17 Gratton and Scott 2016, p. 206.

3 Who gets the job?

1 Curt Rice, 'How McKinsey's Story Became Sheryl Sandberg's statistic – And Why It Didn't Deserve To', *The Huffington Post*, 24 April 2014,

<www.huffingtonpost.co.uk/curt-rice/how-mckinseys-story-became-sheryl-sandbergs-statistic---and-why-it-didnt-deserve-to_b_5198744.html>, accessed 23 December 2016.

2   Stefanie Johnson and David Hekman, 'Women and minorities are penalized for promoting diversity', *Harvard Business Review*, 23 March 2016, <hbr.org/2016/03/women-and-minorities-are-penalized-for-promoting-diversity>, accessed 23 December 2016.

3   Lori Nishiura Mackenzie, 'Vague feedback of "lacks executive presence" is blocking senior women's advancement', *The Huffington Post*, 6 March 2016, <www.huffingtonpost.com/entry/vague-feedback-of-lacks-executive-presence-is-blocking_us_5751c828e4b0da3a3aea6d3d>, accessed 23 December 2016.

4   Robyn Ely, Pamela Stone and Colleen Ammerman, 'Rethink what you "know" about high-achieving women', *Harvard Business Review*, December 2014, <hbr.org/2014/12/rethink-what-you-know-about-high-achieving-women>, accessed 23 December 2016.

5   Weiting Lui, 'These female developers explain how to recruit more female developers', Fast Company, 4 June 2016, <www.fastcompany.com/3058604/strong-female-lead/these-female-developers-explain-how-to-recruit-more-female-developers>, accessed 23 December 2016.

6   Richard Garner, 'Exclusive: Law firm Clifford Chance adopts "CV blind" policy to break Oxbridge recruitment bias', *Independent*, 10 January 2014, <www.independent.co.uk/student/news/exclusive-law-firm-clifford-chance-adopts-cv-blind-policy-to-break-oxbridge-recruitment-bias-9050227.html>, accessed 23 December 2016.

7   Noel Towell, 'Public service goes blind to solve its women problem', *Canberra Times*, 2 June 2016, <www.canberratimes.com.au/national/public-service/public-service-goes-blind-to-solve-its-women-problem-20160531-gp85s4.html>, accessed 23 December 2016.

8   Fiona Smith, 'Anonymous recruitment aims to stamp out bias but can it prevent discrimination?', *The Guardian*, 5 July 2016, <www.theguardian.com/sustainable-business/2016/jul/05/blind-recruitment-aims-to-stamp-out-bias-but-can-it-prevent-discrimination>, accessed 23 December 2016.

9   Usman Chohan, 'Should Australia consider name-blind resumes?', *The Australian*, 12 March 2016, <www.theaustralian.com.au/business/business-spectator/should-australia-consider-nameblind-resumes/news-story/7718bdf109ac7b2ce86d403166e0ead2>, accessed 23 December 2016.

10 Martin Parkinson, 'Workplace diversity is the enemy of stale thinking says Martin Parkinson', *Australian Financial Review*, 2 March 2016, <www.afr.com/opinion/columns/workplace-diversity-the-enemy-of-stale-thinking-says-martin-parkinson-20160301-gn7m9a#ixzz47luPOCOe>, accessed 23 December 2016.

11   Tony Boyd, 'CEOs say redefining merit is the key to promoting women',
      Australian Financial Review, 24 August 2016, <www.afr.com/leadership/
      ceos-say-redefining-merit-is-the-key-to-promoting-women-20160810-
      gqpbls#ixzz4MIfShM3x>, accessed 23 December 2016.
12   Emilio J. Castilla and Stephen Benard, 'The Paradox of Meritocracy in
      Organizations', *Administrative Science Quarterly* 55 (2010): 543–576.
      © 2010 by Johnson Graduate School, Cornell University.

4   Earning power

1   Hilary Osborne, 'Boys get more pocket money than girls', *The Guardian*,
      3 June 2016, <www.theguardian.com/money/2016/jun/03/boys-get-more-
      pocket-money-than-girls-halifax-survey-finds>, accessed 23 December
      2016.
2   Yolanda Beattie, 'The gender pay gap isn't apples for apples but it's still
      gendered', LinkedIn 14 April 2016, <www.linkedin.com/pulse/gender-
      pay-gap-isnt-apples-its-still-gendered-yolanda-beattie?trk=hp-feed-
      article-title-share>, accessed 23 December 2016.
3   Asaf Levanon, Paula England and Paul Allison, 'Occupational
      Feminization and Pay: Assessing Causal Dynamics Using 1950–2000
      U.S. Census Data', *Oxford Journals Social Forces*, Vol 88, Issue 2, 2009,
      pp. 865–891, <sf.oxfordjournals.org/content/88/2/865.short>, accessed
      23 December 2016.
4   Claire Cann Miller, 'As women take over a male-dominated field, the pay
      drops', *New York Times*, 18 March 2016, <www.nytimes.com/2016/03/20/
      upshot/as-women-take-over-a-male-dominated-field-the-pay-drops.
      html?_r=1>, accessed 23 December 2016.
5   Trade Union Congress, 'Fathers working full-time earn 21% more than
      men without children, says TUC', 25 April 2016, <www.tuc.org.uk/
      equality-issues/gender-equality/equal-pay/pregnancy-discrimination/
      fathers-working-full-time-earn-21>, accessed 23 December 2016.
6   Leah Ruppanner, 'We can reduce gender inequality in housework; here's
      how', *The Conversation*, 26 May 2016, <theconversation.com/we-can-we-
      reduce-gender-inequality-in-housework-heres-how-58130>, accessed
      23 December 2016.
7   Australian Bureau of Statistics 2006, *How Australians use their time*, cat.
      no. 4153.0, ABS, Canberra.
8   Ruppanner, 2016.
9   Workplace Gender Equality Agency, 'Gender Equity Insights 2016: Inside
      Australia's Gender Pay Gap', *BCEC/ WGEA Gender Equity Series*, 2016,

<www.wgea.gov.au/.../BCEC_WGEA_Gender_Pay_Equity_Insight>, accessed 23 December 2016.

10   Adam Galinsky and Maurice Schweitzer, 'It's good to be the Queen...but it's easier being the King', McKinsey&Company, September 2015, <www.mckinsey.com/global-themes/leadership/its-good-to-be-the-queen-but-its-easier-being-the-king>, accessed 23 December 2016.

11   Galinsky and Schweitzer 2015.

12   Gloria Feldt, 'Actually, women do ask for raises as often as men – they just don't get them', Fast Company, 10 November 2016, <www.fastcompany.com/3065461/strong-female-lead/actually-women-do-ask-for-raises-as-often-as-men-they-just-dont-get-them>, accessed 23 December 2016.

13   Meraiah Foley, 'Becoming a "mumpreneur" is an option of last resort for many working mothers', The Sydney Morning Herald 4 May 2016, <www.smh.com.au/comment/becoming-a-mumpreneur-is-an-option-of-last-resort-for-many-working-mothers-20160504-golrkl.html>, accessed 23 December 2016.

14   WGEA, 'Employers lift their game on pay equity', WGEA media release, 2 October 2015, <www.wgea.gov.au/media-releases/employers-lift-their-game-pay-equity>, accessed 23 December 2016.

15   WGEA, 'Employers reminded to report on gender equity', WGEA media release, 26 May 2016, <www.wgea.gov.au/sites/default/files/media_release_reporting_reminder.pdf>, accessed 23 December 2016.

16   WGEA, '2015 Pay Equity Report Card: In Your Hands', WGEA, 2015, <inyourhands.org.au/>, accessed 23 December 2016.

17   WGEA, 'Case study: Research showcasing leading practice at the Commonwealth Bank', September 2015, <www.wgea.gov.au/sites/default/files/Commonwealth_Bank_Pay_Equity_Casestudy.PDF>, accessed 23 December 2016.

18   Susan Muldowney, 'Money talks: Australia's persistent gender pay gap', HRMOnline, 2 November 2015, <www.hrmonline.com.au/section/featured/money-talks-australias-persistent-gender-pay-gap/>, accessed 23 December 2016.

19   Agnes King, 'KPMG Australia reveals gender pay gap data', Australian Financial Review, 8 September 2015, <www.afr.com/business/accounting/kpmg-australia-reveals-gender-pay-gap-data-20150907-gjh6pl>, accessed 23 December 2016.

20   Westpac, 'Gender barriers restrict women in small business', Westpac Media Release, 20 May 2015, <www.westpac.com.au/about-westpac/media/media-releases/2015/20-may-15>, accessed 23 December 2016.

21   Karyn Loscocco and Joyce Robinson, 'Barriers to Women's Small Business Success in the United States', Gender and Society, 5 (4),

December 1991, pp. 511–532, <gas.sagepub.com/content/5/4/511.
abstract>, accessed 23 December 2016.

22 AWCCI, 'National Research findings: Women are shaping the new
economy', AWCCI media release, March 2012, <www.awcci.org.
au/news/
media-releases/12-media-release/70-national-research-findings-women-
are-shaping-the-new-economy.html>, accessed 23 December 2016.

23 Office of Women, 'Profile of Australian women in business', Australian
Bureau of Statistics, 2015, <www.dpmc.gov.au/sites/default/files/
publications/profile_of_australian_women_in_business_0.pdf>,
accessed 23 December 2016.

24 Springboard Enterprises, 'History of Springboard', 2015, <sb.co/about/
history/>, accessed 23 December 2016.

25 Topaz Conway, 'Why female entrepreneurs struggle to access capital',
SmartCompany, 31 March 2015, <www.smartcompany.com.au/finance/
funding/46289-why-female-entrepreneurs-struggle-to-access-capital/>,
accessed 23 December 2016.

26 Senate Standing Committee on Economics, 'A husband is not a
retirement plan: Achieving economic security for women in retirement
report', Senate Economics Reference Committee, April 2016,
<www.aph.gov.au/Parliamentary_Business/Committees/Senate/
Economics/Economic_security_for_women_in_retirement/Report>,
accessed 23 December 2016.

27 Meraiah Foley, 2016.

28 Shalailah Medhora, 'Low-paid women have 42% less super than men on
same income, data shows', The Guardian, 5 April 2016,
<www.theguardian.com/australia-news/2016/apr/05/low-paid-women-
have-42-less-super-than-men-on-same-income-data-shows>, accessed
23 December 2016.

29 Stephen Dubner, 'The true story of the gender pay gap', 7 January 2016,
<freakonomics.com/podcast/the-true-story-of-the-gender-pay-gap-a-
new-freakonomics-radio-podcast/>, accessed 23 December 2016.

5 How targets build meritocracies

1 Nassim Khadem, 'Australia will not hit 30% women on boards by 2018,
time for quotas: Elizabeth Proust', The Sydney Morning Herald, 8 June
2016, <smh.com.au/business/workplace-relations/australia-will-not-
hit-30-women-on-boards-by-2018-time-for-quotas-elizabeth-proust-
20160607-gpdd80.html#ixzz4C7ZYW4Z4>, accessed 23 December 2016.

2 Nassim Khadem, 'Gender reporting is not red tape: Parkinson',
Australian Financial Review, 27 February 2014, <www.afr.com/news/

policy/tax/gender-reporting-is-not-red-tapeparkinson-20140227-ixouk#ixzz4CbjsK81g>, accessed 23 December 2016.

3   Sally Freeman and Ben Travers, 'ASX companies fall short in gender diversity and risk reporting', KPMG Newsroom, 1 June 2016, <newsroom.kpmg.com.au/?p=3863>, accessed 23 December 2016.

4   Harley Dennett, 'David Morrison on diversity targets and making change the hard way', *Women's Agenda*, 28 January 2016, <www.womensagenda.com.au/talking-about/top-stories/item/6703-david-morrison-on-diversity-targets-and-making-change-the-hard-way>, accessed 23 December 2016.

5   Sean Farrell, 'Gender pay gap has barely improved in four years, say MPs', *The Guardian*, 22 March 2016, <www.theguardian.com/world/2016/mar/22/gender-pay-gap-has-barely-shrunk-in-four-years-say-mps>, accessed 23 December 2016.

6   Castilla, Emilio J. and Stephen Benard, 'The Paradox of Meritocracy in Organizations', *Administrative Science Quarterly* 55 (2010): 543–576. © 2010 by Johnson Graduate School, Cornell University.

7   Victor Sojo, Robert Wood, Sally Wood and Melissa Wheeler, 'Reporting requirements, targets and quotas for women in leadership', *The Leadership Quarterly*, vol. 27, issue 3, June 2016, pp. 519–536, <www.sciencedirect.com/science/article/pii/S1048984315001514>, accessed 23 December 2016.

8   Conrad Liveris, 'Women on boards: men must lead by example in debate on gender diversity', *Australian Financial Review*, 13 June 2015, <www.afr.com/opinion/columns/women-on-boards-men-must-lead-by-example-in-debate-on-gender-diversity-20150713-gib22k>, accessed 23 December 2016.

9   Sarah Gordon, 'Women bosses boost female places in boardroom', *Financial Times*, 21 November 2016, <www.ft.com/content/afd30286-ab5b-11e6-9cb3-bb8207902122>, accessed 23 December 2016.

10 Ursula Malone, 'Number of women on ASX 200 company boards soaring, report shows', ABC, 16 June 2016, <www.abc.net.au/news/2016-06-16/number-of-women-on-asx-200-company-boards-increasing/7517156>, accessed 23 December 2016.

11 Cordelia Fine, 'Status Quota', *The Monthly*, 29 March 2012, <www.themonthly.com.au/issue/2012/march/1330562640/cordelia-fine/status-quota>, accessed 23 December 2016.

12 Our Watch, 'Understanding Violence: Facts and figures', <www.ourwatch.org.au/Understanding-Violence/Facts-and-figures>, accessed 23 December 2016.

13 Eli Greenblatt, 'Ahmed Fahour: gender inequality depressing; make firms fix it', *The Australian*, 11 October 2016, <www.theaustralian.com.au/

business/financial-services/ahmed-fahour-gender-inequality-depressing-make-firms-fix-it/news-story/c6136e63dcd597a813de891edddd04a2>, accessed 23 December 2016.

14   Vivian Hunt, Dennis Layton and Sara Prince, 'Why diversity matters', *McKinsey Quarterly*, January 2015, <www.mckinsey.com/business-functions/organization/our-insights/why-diversity-matters>, accessed 23 December 2016.

15   Ellen Wulfhorst, 'Half of women on boards like quotas but male colleagues say no – survey', Reuters, 22 April 2016, <in.mobile.reuters.com/article/idINKCN0XI0WV?irpc=932>, accessed 23 December 2016.

16   Cathrine Selerstad, Morten Huse and Silvija Seres, 'Lessons from Norway in getting women onto corporate boards', *The Conversation*, 7 March 2015, <theconversation.com/lessons-from-norway-in-getting-women-onto-corporate-boards-38338>, accessed 23 December 2016.

17   Selerstad, Huse and Seres, 2015.

18   Aaron Dhir, *Challenging Boardroom Homogeneity*, Cambridge University Press, Cambridge, 2012.

19   Aaron Dhir, 'What Norway can teach the US about getting more women into boardrooms', *The Atlantic*, 4 May 2015, <www.theatlantic.com/business/archive/2015/05/what-norway-can-teach-the-us-about-getting-more-women-into-boardrooms/392195/>, accessed 23 December 2016.

20   Oliver Staley, 'You know those quotas for female board members in Europe? They're working', *Quartz*, 3 May 2015, <qz.com/674276/you-know-those-quotas-for-female-board-members-in-europe-theyre-working/>, accessed 23 December 2016.

21   Bjorn Lindahl, 'Norway's female boardroom quotas; what has been the effect?', *Nordic Labour Journal*, 21 May 2015, <www.nordiclabourjournal.org/artikler/forskning/research-2015/article.2015-05-20.3011019632>, accessed 23 December 2016.

6   Promotions not panaceas

1   Francesca Gino, 'Ending gender discrimination requires more than a training program', *Harvard Business Review*, 10 October 2014, <hbr.org/2014/10/ending-gender-discrimination-requires-more-than-a-training-program>, accessed 23 December 2016.

2   Grant Robertson and Margaret Byrne, 'Getting gender balance "unstuck": Taking action with a new strategic approach', *Governance Directions*, March 2016, <www.governanceinstitute.com.au/media/867025/gender_balance_senior_management_march_2016.pdf>, accessed 23 December 2016.

3   Jennifer De Vries, 'Mentoring for change', *Universities Australia Executive Women/LH Martin Institute*, March 2011, <www.lhmartininstitute.edu.au/userfiles/files/2011_UAEW_mentoringforchangereport.pdf>, accessed 23 December 2016.

4   Cynthia Cockburn, *In the Way of Women: Men's Resistance to Sex Equality in Organizations*, ILR Press, New York, 1991. Robin Ely and Debra Meyerson, 'Theories of Gender in Organizations: A New Approach to Organizational Analysis and Change', *Research in Organizational Behaviour*, vol. 22, 2000, pp. 103–151. Debra Meyerson and Joyce Fletcher, 'A Modest Manifesto for Shattering the Glass Ceiling', *Harvard Business Review*, vol. 78, no. 1, 2000, pp. 126–136.

5   Nicola Woolcock, 'Female mentors fight sexism in the city', *The Sunday Times*, 16 April 2016, <www.thetimes.co.uk/edition/news/mentors-go-to-work-on-sexist-bosses-d6thwt5qn>, accessed 23 December 2016.

6   Emily Cadman, 'The secret of success is to be sponsored, not over-mentored', *Financial Times*, 15 September 2015, <www.ft.com/cms/s/0/2728fe36-4a7c-11e5-b558-8a9722977189.html#ixzz46CCcJnb1i>, accessed 23 December 2016.

7   Gino, 2014.

8   Frank Dobbin and Alexandra Kalev, 'Try and Make Me! Why Corporate Diversity Training Fails', Massachusetts Institute of Technology Sloan School for Business, 17 March 2016, <mitsloan.mit.edu/iwer/wp-content/uploads/2015/04/AATraining-3-16-2015-clean.pdf>, accessed 23 December 2016.

9   Frank Dobbin and Alexandra Kalev, 'Why diversity programs fail', *Harvard Business Review*, July/August 2016, <hbr.org/2016/07/why-diversity-programs-fail?utm_campaign=harvardbiz&utm_source=twitter&utm_medium=social>, accessed 23 December 2016.

10 David Miller, 'Tech companies spend big money on bias training – but it hasn't improved diversity numbers', *The Conversation*, 10 July 2015, <www.usnews.com/news/articles/2015/07/29/can-bias-training-really-improve-diversity-in-tech>, accessed 23 December 2016.

11 Miller, *The Conversation*, 2015.

12 Joanna Lublin, 'Bringing hidden biases into the light', *Wall St Journal*, 9 January 2014, <www.wsj.com/articlesSB10001424052702303754404579308562690896896>, accessed 23 December 2016.

13 Melissa Thomas-Hunt and Carlos Santos, 'Everybody's biased, so I can be too', *Darden Ideas to Action*, 5 November 2015, <ideas.darden.virginia.edu/2015/11/everybodys-biased-so-i-can-be-too/>, accessed 23 December 2016.

14 Laura Bates, 'What use are women's networks? We need less talk and more action from businesses', *The Guardian*, 25 March 2016, <www. theguardian.com/lifeandstyle/2016/mar/25/what-use-are-womens-networks-we-need-less-talk-and-more-action-from-businesses>, accessed 23 December 2016.

7 Military manouvres: An army of women

1 John Kerin, 'Digger mythology worries Army chief', *Australian Financial Review*, 24–27 April 2014.

2 David Morrison, 'United Nations International Women's Day conference address', 8–9 March 2013, <our work/speeches/army.gov.au>, accessed 23 December 2016.

3 David Morrison, 'Chief of Army Lieutenant General David Morrison message about unacceptable behaviour', 8 March 2012, <www.youtube. com/watch?v=QaqpoeVgr8U>, accessed 23 December 2016.

4 Defence People Group, 'Women in the ADF 2015/16 Report', Department of Defence, December 2016, <www.defence.gov.au/annualreports/15-16/ Downloads/Women-in-ADF-Report-2015-16-online-only.pdf>, accessed 23 December 2016.

5 Megan MacKenzie, *Beyond the Band of Brothers: The US military and the myth that women can't fight*, Cambridge University Press, Cambridge, 2015.

6 Julie McKay, 'Exploring effective strategies to engage women in leadership roles in non-traditional sectors', *Churchill Fellowship Report*, 8 May 2015, <www.churchilltrust.com.au/media/fellows/McKay_Julie__ Effective_strategies_to_engage_women_in_leadership_roles.pdf>, accessed 23 December 2016.

8 Backlash and confidence tricks

1 Danielle Paquette, 'Why young women are less likely to push for a pay rise', *The Sydney Morning Herald*, 8 July 2016, <www.smh.com.au/ business/workplace-relations/why-young-women-are-less-likely-to-push-for-a-pay-rise-20160707-gq15dm.html#ixzz4EcgtbxpV>, accessed 23 December 2016.

2 Bob Brown, 'Lack of confidence proving to be real killer for women in technology', *Network World*, 14 April 2016, <www.cio.com/ article/3056753/careers-staffing/lack-of-confidence-proving-to-be-real-killer-for-women-in-technology.html>, accessed 23 December 2016.

3 Jessica Irvine, '"She didn't ask for it": Is this why women don't get the top job?', *The Sydney Morning Herald*, 25 July 2016, <www.smh.com.au/business/she-didnt-ask-for-it-is-this-why-women-dont-get-the-top-job-20160724-gqck04.html>, accessed 23 December 2016.

4 Mary Beard, 'The public voice of women', *London Review of Books*, 20 March 2014, <www.lrb.co.uk/v36/n06/mary-beard/the-public-voice-of-women>, accessed 23 December 2016.

5 Elizabeth Thomson, 'Battling with words', Department of Defence, February 2014, <www.defence.gov.au/adc/publications/commanders/2014/battling_with_words_web.pdf>, accessed 23 December 2016.

6 Deborah Cameron, *The Myth of Mars and Venus: Do men and women really speak different languages?*, Oxford University Press, Oxford, 2007.

7 Louann Brizendine, *The Female Brain*, Broadway Books, New York, 2006.

8 Cameron 2007, p. 119.

9 Deborah Cameron, 'Sorry, but it's complicated', *Language: a feminist guide blog*, 28 July 2016, <debuk.wordpress.com/2016/07/28/sorry-but-its-complicated/>, accessed 23 December 2016.

10 Deborah Cameron, 'Just don't do it', *Language: a feminist guide blog*, 5 July 2015, <debuk.wordpress.com/2015/07/05/just-dont-do-it/>, accessed 23 December 2016.

11 Staff writer, 'Hollywood says men more important as they age, but women less', *The Sydney Morning Herald*, 20 April 2016, <www.smh.com.au/entertainment/movies/hollywood-says-men-more-important-as-they-age-but-women-less-20160420-goaqmu.html#ixzz46TUUyVVy>, accessed 23 December 2016.

12 Screen Australia, 'Gender Matters', 7 December 2015, <www.screenaustralia.gov.au/new-directions/gender-matters>, accessed 23 December 2016.

13 Gaven Morris, 'A balanced media? Not when it comes to gender', *The Drum*, 8 March 2016, <www.abc.net.au/news/2016-03-08/morris-a-balanced-media-not-when-it-comes-to-gender/7228262>, accessed 23 December 2016.

14 SkillPad Australia, '2013 Women in Media Report', *The Women's Leadership Institute Australia*, 2013, <www.wlia.org.au/wp-content/uploads/2015/04/WLIA-Skillpad-2013-Report.pdf>, accessed 23 December 2016.

15 Staff writer, 'Who do journos listen to?', *New Matilda*, 13 June 2013, <newmatilda.com/2013/06/13/who-do-journos-listen/>, accessed 23 December 2016.

16 Julia Baird, 'How to explain mansplaining', *New York Times*, 21 April 2016, <www.nytimes.com/2016/04/21/opinion/how-to-explain-

mansplaining.html?smid=nytcore-ipad-share&smprod=nytcore-ipad&_
r=1>, accessed 23 December 2016.

17 Sheryl Sandberg and Adam Grant, 'Speaking while female', *New York
Times*, 1 November 2015, <www.nytimes.com/2015/01/11/opinion/
sunday/speaking-while-female.html?_r=0>, accessed 23 December 2016.

18 Hans Schulz, 'Why I say no to all male panels', *Washington Post*,
13 October 2015, <www.washingtonpost.com/posteverything/
wp/2015/10/13/why-i-say-no-to-all-male-panels/>, accessed 23 December
2016.

19 Darren Hill, 'How to avoid a "manel": Panel Pledge signee Darren Hill
offers 3 ways to do it', *Australian Financial Review*, 11 May 2016, <www.
afr.com/leadership/how-to-avoid-a-manel-panel-pledge-signee-darren-
hill-offers-3-ways-to-do-it-2016>, accessed 23 December 2016.

20 Graham Staines, Carol Tavris and Toby Epstein Jayaratne, 'The queen
bee syndrome', *Psychology Today* 7(1), 1974.

21 Sheryl Sandberg and Adam Grant, 'The myth of the catty woman',
New York Times, 23 June 2016, <mobile.nytimes.com/2016/06/23/
opinion/sunday/sheryl-sandberg-on-the-myth-of-the-catty-woman.
html?referer=http://m.facebook.com>, accessed 23 December 2016.

22 Emma Gray, 'Queen Bee syndrome false: women help other women
advance in the workforce, study', *The Huffington Post*, 12 June 2012,
<www.catalyst.org/knowledge/high-potentials-pipeline-leaders-pay-
it-forward> and <www.huffingtonpost.com/2012/06/12/queen-bee-
syndrome-women-workplace-catalyst_n_1588604.html>, accessed
23 December 2016.

23 Natalia Karelia and Laura Guillén, 'Me, a woman, and a leader: Positive
social identity and identity conflict', *Organisational Behaviour and
Human Decision Processes*, 125, 2014, pp. 204–219.

24 Aimee Hanson, 'Show me how to lead like a woman: why positive gender
identity matters in leadership', *The Glass Hammer*, 12 March 2015,
<theglasshammer.com/2015/03/12/show-me-how-to-lead-like-a-woman-
why-positive-gender-identity-matters-in-leadership/>, accessed
23 December 2016.

25 Sharon Mavin, 'Venus envy: problematizing solidarity behaviour and
queen bees', *Women in Management Review*, Vol. 21 Iss. 4, 2006,
pp. 264–276.

Conclusion: And where to from here?

1 AFP News Agency, 'Crash dummies: sexist car safety features injure
women', *News.com.au*, 21 October 2011, <www.news.com.au/technology/

crash-dummies-sexist-car-safety-features-injure-women/story-
e6frfro0-1226172707362>, accessed 23 December 2016.

2   Australian Women Donors Network, 'Gender-Wise Toolkit for
    Grantmakers', Australian Women Donors Network, 17 December 2015,
    <AWDN_Toolkit_2015_v5.pdf >, accessed 23 December 2016.

3   Eli Greenblat, 'Ahmed Fahour: Gender inequality depressing; make firms
    fix it', *The Australian*, 11 October 2016, <www.theaustralian.com.au/
    business/financial-services/ahmed-fahour-gender-inequality-depressing-
    make-firms-fix-it/news-story/c6136e63dcd597a813de891edddd04a2>,
    accessed 23 December 2016.

4   William Bielby, 'Gender & Work: challenging conventional wisdom',
    Harvard Business School, 2013, <www.hbs.edu/faculty/conferences/
    2013-w50-research-symposium/Documents/bielby.pdf>, accessed
    23 December 2016.

5   Clementine Ford, 'This is what equality looks like', *Daily Life*, 14 June
    2016, <www.dailylife.com.au/news-and-views/this-is-what-equality-
    looks-like-20160613-gphyt3.html>, accessed 23 December 2016.

6   Cordelia Fine, 'Are men and women really that different?', ABC
    Radio National, 12 January 2016, <radio.abc.net.au/programitem/
    pg0JGOZrB7?play=true>, accessed 23 December 2016.

7   Gaby Hinsliff, 'The power of one: how single women are reshaping the
    political landscape', *The Guardian*, 22 March 2016, <www.theguardian.
    com/lifeandstyle/2016/mar/21/single-women-reshaping-political-
    landscape-rebecca-traister-all-the-single-ladies-unmarried>, accessed
    23 December 2016.

8   Deborah Cameron, *The Myth of Mars and Venus: Do men and women
    really speak different languages?*, Oxford University Press, Oxford, 2007,
    p. 181.

Index